Memoir of NATHANIEL BOWDITCH

BY

NATHANIEL INGERSOLL BOWDITCH

APPLEWOOD BOOKS
Carlisle, Massachusetts

Memoir of Nathaniel Bowditch was originally published in 1841.

ISBN: 978-1-4290-9745-1

Prepared for Publication by HP

MEMOIR

OF

NATHANIEL BOWDITCH.

PREPARED FOR THE YOUNG.

" The House in which he lived." — P. 3

PRINTED FOR THE WARREN STREET CHAPEL.

BOSTON:

JAMES MUNROE AND COMPANY.

1841.

INFLUENCED by feelings I could scarcely comprehend, while, at the same time they were most sweet to me, I was induced to address the pupils of the WARREN STREET CHAPEL, on the Sunday afternoon after my father died. The subjects were his life and serene departure from this world. I am aware, that some of my nearest friends thought ·it strange that my heart, on the occasion of his death, was so tinged with joyousness. To them I could merely say, that an event so calm suggested to me nought of sadness. I wished my young companions should feel as I did, and that in their minds, a quiet death following a good life should be clothed with beauty, and that they might feel assured, moreover, that in accordance with the Scotch proverb, " A gude life makes a gude end." A gentleman who was present during the address, and who is deeply interested in the education of the young, requested me to prepare for his Journal a sketch similar to that I had spoken. In accordance with that desire, a Memoir was prepared, and after its publication the WARREN STREET CHAPEL ASSOCIATION requested that it should be put, with some revision, into this form. And now, as it was originally spoken for them,

I   DEDICATE

IT

TO THE GIRLS AND BOYS OF WARREN STREET CHAPEL.

PREFACE.

———

FOUR years since the Teachers of the WAR-
REN STREET CHAPEL published a volume about
the size of this, containing a Memoir of that
excellent youth, JAMES JACKSON, JR. The
public has fully shown that it regarded the
undertaking with pleasure.

Since that time the Teachers have given,
through Retzsch's vivid Outlines, a specimen of
the very poetry of engraving, in the " GAME
OF LIFE," or the struggles of a pure soul against
the Principle of Evil, in this world.

In accordance with their implied promise,
when publishing Jackson's Memoir, they now

present the life of a just man. He commenced
his career with energy and truth, and passing
through it with constant hopefulness, closed it
with a calm and happy death.   They trust that
this last may be a fit companion for the other
volume.   In the first they strewed flowers upon the grave of early youth ; in this, they hope
to offer a like tribute to white-haired and venerable age.   Both have the same object, viz.
the improvement of the young.

   Boston, Dec. 24, 1840.

CONTENTS.

CHAPTER I.

CHAPTER II.

CHAPTER III.

[From 1784 to 1796, — aged 10 — 22.]

CHAPTER IV.

[From 1796 to 1797, — aged 23 — 24.]

CHAPTER V.

[From 1797 to 1800, — aged 24 — 27.]

CHAPTER VI.

———

CHAPTER VII.

CHAPTER VIII.

[From 1803 to 1817 — aged 30 — 44.]

CHAPTER IX.

[*From* 1803 *to* 1823, — *aged* 30 — 50.]

CHAPTER X.

CHAPTER XI.

CHAPTER XII.

MEMOIR.

MEMOIR.

CHAPTER I.

[*From 1773 to 1784 — under ten years of age.*]

Birth. — Childhood.

NATHANIEL BOWDITCH, whose history I shall relate to you, was one whose character and actions presented many circumstances which, I think, cannot fail of being interesting to you. He died, a short time ago, here, in Boston; and, from having been a poor and ignorant boy, became a man known all over the world, for his great learning, while at the same time he was beloved for the goodness of his heart and the integrity of his character. May the perusal of his history excite some of you to imitate his virtues and his energy.

He was born in Salem, a town about fourteen miles from Boston, the capital city of our
State of Massachusetts. His birthday was
March 26th, 1773. His father was at first a
cooper, and afterwards a shipmaster. He and
his wife were exceedingly poor, and they had
many children. Nathaniel was the fourth
child. He had two sisters and three brothers.
When he was about two and a half years old,
his parents removed to a very small wooden
house in Danvers, only three miles, however,
from Salem ; and here the boy attended school
for the first time, and began to show those gen-
erous feelings, and that love of learning, which
he displayed so much in after-life. The old
schoolhouse is still standing, in which he

studied the alphabet, and learned to spell and
read. It is an old-fashioned building, with a

long slanting roof, which, at the back of the house, nearly reaches the ground. Its single chimney, with many curious and pretty corners, still rises in the middle of the roof, as it did sixty years ago. Around the dwelling is a grass plat, upon which he used, when a child like yourselves, to play heartily with his schoolmates. It is now planted with shrubs, such as the farmers most need. The house in which he lived was nearly opposite that in which the school was kept. It had but two rooms in it, and all its furniture was of the simplest kind.

I visited the relations of the schoolmistress. She died many, many years ago ; but her niece, when I asked about Nathaniel, told me how her aunt used to love him, for his earnestness in pursuing his studies, and for his gentleness, while under her care. He was "a nice boy," she was wont to say. While in Danvers, his father was most of the time at sea, he having been obliged to give up his trade and become a sailor, when the Revolutionary War broke out.*

---

* You will know better, by and by, about the Revolutionary War. I will merely state now, that this war was between America and Great Britain, in order to free ourselves from the power of England. The reason why the

He lived, during his father's absence, very happily with his mother and his brothers and sisters. During the whole of his after-life, he used to delight to go near the small house in which he had dwelt so pleasantly. The family was " a family of love." He had a brother William, to whom he was peculiarly attached. He was more grave and sober than Nathaniel ; for the latter, with all his devotion to study, was full of fun, frolic, and good nature. But William was equally, and perhaps more, gentle. The brothers frequently studied together from an old family Bible ; and on Sundays, when they were quite small, their grandmother, who was a very excellent woman, used to place this large book, with its wooden covers and bright brazen clasps, upon the foot of her bed ; and hour after hour did those two boys trace, with their fin-

British King had any thing to do with America was this. Many years ago, a number of people came over from England, and settled in this country; and of course the small colony needed the aid of the government from which it originated. After a time, the people here wanted to govern themselves, and they therefore went to battle about it, because England would not grant them all their wishes. This contest, which lasted for several years, was terminated by the freedom of the United States.

gers upon the map, the forty years' wanderings
of the Israelites, before they came in to the long-
looked-for land of Canaan. I have said that
Nathaniel frequently went to look upon the
house in which he had lived, and so did he
often call upon the family in which this old
Bible was kept, in order that he might see the
volume which he had so loved to pore over,
when a boy. It reminded him of the delightful
home of his childhood, where his dear and worthy mother used to endeavor to make him good,
in order that he might become an honor to her
and to the people. His mother was one who
was extremely kind, yet she was by no means
afraid to correct her children, if she found them
erring. Nathaniel sometimes suffered, because,
like every boy, he sometimes did wrong; but
generally, the mother found that he could be
easily guided by her love. I seem to see her
now, taking her little son, and leading him to
the window of the cottage in Danvers, to see
the beautiful new moon just setting in the west ;
while, at the same time, she kisses and blesses
him, and talks to him of his absent father, and
they both send up earnest wishes for his safe
and speedy return. She was very careful to

instil into all her children the importance of
truth. " Speak the truth always, my boy,"
said she. She likewise loved religion, and she
was very liberal in her feelings towards those
who differed from her upon this subject. Nev-
ertheless, believing that the Episcopal kind of
worship was the most correct, she educated all
her children in that form. An anecdote, which
Nathaniel, when he became a man, frequently
related, will show you how much influence her
instructions in this particular had upon him.
Among the Episcopalians, the prayers are read
and the people repeat, aloud, some answer.
One day, Nathaniel called his brothers and
sisters around him, and, taking his mother's
book of prayer, with a sober face began to read
aloud from it, while his brothers made the an-
swers. They had continued some minutes
amusing themselves in this way, when their
mother entered the room. She was very much
troubled, at first, as she supposed they were
ridiculing the services she held as sacred. " My
sons," said she, " I am pleased to see you read
that book ; but you should never do so in a
careless manner." Her feelings were relieved,
by their assuring her they meant no disrespect.

The family was very poor; so poor, indeed, that sometimes they had nothing to eat for several successive days, but common coarse bread, with perhaps a little pork. Wheaten bread was almost never allowed any one of them. Their clothing, too, was at times very thin. Frequently, during the whole winter, the boys wore their summer jackets and trousers. At times, his schoolmates used to laugh at our young friend, because he wore such a thin dress when they were thickly clad in winter garments. But he never was afraid of their merriment, nor made angry by it; on the contrary, he laughed heartily at them, for supposing him unable to bear the cold. He knew that no good would be gained by complaints, and that he would distress his mother if he made any; he therefore bore contentedly his want of clothing, and sought even to make himself merry with those who ridiculed him.

At the age of seven years, and after returning to Salem, he went to a school kept by a man named Watson. Master Watson was one who had sufficient learning for those times; though the boys who now go to school in Boston would think it very strange, if a master did

not attempt to teach more than he did. None
of the scholars had a dictionary. Master Watson was a good man, but he suffered much from
headache, and therefore he was frequently liable
to violent fits of anger, and, when thus excited,
as it generally happens in such cases, he was
guilty of injustice. An instance of this, young
Bowditch met with, not long after he entered
the school. From early life, he had loved
ciphering, or arithmetic ; and thinking that at
school, he would be able to learn something
more about this than he had previously gained
from his brothers, while at home, during the
long winter evenings, he requested the master to
allow him to study it. As he seemed too young,
this request was not granted. But, being determined to study what pleased him so much, he
obtained a letter from his father, in which Mr.
Bowditch requested Mr. Watson to allow his
son to pursue his favorite study. The schoolmaster, on receiving the message, was very angry, and said to his pupil, " Very well. I'll
give you a sum that will satisfy you ; " and immediately prepared a question that he thought
Nathaniel would be unable to answer, and
which he could not have answered had he not

studied at home. But the boy had learned
before, sufficiently to enable him to perform
the task; and, having done so, he ran gaily to
the desk, expecting to be praised for his proper
performance of duty. You may imagine his
surprise at being saluted with these words;
" You little rascal, who shewed you how to do
this sum? I shall punish you for attempting to
deceive me." The poor lad's heart swelled and
beat violently. He blushed and trembled, from
fear of punishment; but still more at the suspicion which his instructer had expressed, that
he had been guilty of telling a lie. Filled with
contending emotions, he stammered out, " I did
it, sir." But his master would not believe
him, and was about to strike him, when an elder
brother interfered, and stated that Nathaniel
knew very well how to perform the task, for he
himself had previously taught him enough to enable him to do it. Our young arithmetician
thus escaped the punishment; but he never
could forget that he had been accused of falsehood. His pious and truth-loving mother had
so firmly fastened in his mind the holiness of
truth, that he never thought of deviating from
it; and, during his life, he considered that any

one, who even suspected him of falsehood, had done him the greatest injury. How well it would be, if all of our boys loved truth as he did !

This was the only serious difficulty he met with, while at this school. He was the same lively lad at every thing he undertook, that he had been previously. He was beloved by his comrades, for his good nature, and was always engaged in useful employment or innocent amusements. When he was about ten years of age, his father became poorer than ever ; and moreover, in consequence of loss of regular employment and of the little property which he possessed, he gave himself up to habits of intoxication. From having been a brave man, he became a coward ; and, unable to look at the distress of his family, made their poverty many times more burdensome, by habits which wholly unfitted him for active duties. Under these circumstances, his son, at the age of ten years and three months, left school, and soon afterwards was bound an apprentice to Messrs. Ropes and Hodges, who kept a ship-chandler's shop.

As this was one of the important times in his life, I think I will finish this chapter with only two remarks, for the boys and girls who may be reading this. You see a boy, who, before he was ten years old, showed great love of truth ; great perseverance ; intense love of study, particularly of ciphering ; and lastly, you perceive him under the influence of a good mother, who devoted herself to exciting in him all just and holy sentiments ; particularly does she point out to him truth as one grand aim of his existence. Now, I wish you to remember these facts, and see where they eventually lead him; and if you remember, you may be induced to imitate him, in some respects.

CHAPTER II.

DOUBTLESS, it was with a sorrowing heart
that Nathaniel left his own dear home, and his
kind mother, to take up his abode among strangers ; for he was to live at the house of his employer, Mr. Hodges. But, if he did feel sad, he
was not one to neglect a duty in consequence
of sorrow. The shop in which he was employed was situated very near the wharves, in the
lower part of the town of Salem. We do not
see many such stores now, in Boston ; though
something similar is sometimes found in small
country towns. In it, a great variety of goods
was sold, especially every thing which would be
useful to a sailor. Pork and nails, hammers
and butter, were kept in adjacent barrels. The

walls were hung with all the tools needed in the seafaring life. There was a long counter in it, at one end of which, Nathaniel had his little desk ; when not engaged with customers, he used to read and write there. He always kept a slate by his side ; and, when not occupied by the duties of the shop, he was busied with his favorite pursuit of arithmetic. In the warm weather of summer, when there was little business, and the heat was uncomfortable, he was frequently seen by the neighbors ciphering, while his slate rested upon the half-door of the shop ; for in those days the shop-doors were made in two parts, so that frequently the lower half was shut while the upper was open. Thus he was always actively employed, instead of being idle, as is too frequently the case with boys in similar circumstances. Even on the great holydays of Fourth of July and General Training, he did not leave his studies for the purpose of going to see the parade, but remained at the shop, laboring to improve himself; or, if the shop was closed, he was in his little garret-room at his employer's house. Study and reading were beginning to be his only recreation. Frequently, after the store was closed at night, he remained until nine or ten o'clock, instead of spending the evening in folly or guilt. Many long winter nights he passed in a similar manner, at his master's house, by the kitchen fire. While here, he did not become morose or ill-natured, but frequently, when the servant girl wished to go to see her parents, who lived one or two miles off, he took her place by the side of the cradle of his master's child, and rocked it gently with his foot, while busily occupied at his books. This was one of the sweetest incidents in this great man's life. It was the germ of his benevolence in after life. A truly great man is kind-hearted as well as wise. Nathaniel began thus early his course of genuine humanity and science. So must you do if you would imitate him.

As he became older, he became interested in larger and more important works ; and of these, fortunately, he found an abundant supply. His employer lived in the house of Judge Ropes, and Nathaniel had permission to use the library of this gentleman as much as he wished. In this collection he found one set of books, which he ever afterwards valued very much. He sought to purchase a copy of it, when he was

old, having the same kind of feeling towards it
that he bore towards his grandmother's Bible.
It was Chambers's Cyclopedia. As you may
judge from the name Cyclopedia, these books,
consisting of four very large volumes, contained
much upon a great many subjects. It is like a
dictionary. He read every piece in it; and
copied into blank books, which he obtained for
the purpose, every thing he thought particularly
interesting, especially all about ciphering. Previously, he had studied navigation, or the methods
whereby the sailors are enabled to guide their
ships across the ocean. In this Cyclopedia he
found much upon this subject; also upon astronomy, or the knowledge of the stars, and other
heavenly bodies; and upon mensuration, or the
art with which we are enabled to measure large
quantities of land or water.

But he was not satisfied with merely studying
what others did. He made several dials and
curious instruments for measuring the weather,
&c. He likewise, at the age of fourteen years,
made an Almanac, so accurately and minutely
finished, that it might have been published.
Whilst engaged upon this last, he was more
than usually laborious. The first rays of the

morning saw him at labor, and he sat up, with
his rushlight, until late at night. If any asked
where Nathaniel was, the reply was, " He is engaged in making his Almanac." He was just
fourteen years of age, when he finished it. It
is now in existence, and in his library. This
library consists of more than two thousand
books, which, during his long life, he had collected. Yet, to my mind, the little Almanac is
the most valuable book of the whole, because it
was the first evidence he gave of his perseverance of mind.

August 1, 1787, that is, at the age of fourteen, he was introduced to a mode of calculating
which was wholly new to him. His brother
came home from his school, where he had been
learning navigation, and told him that his master
had a mode of ciphering by means of letters.
Nathaniel puzzled himself very much about the
matter, and imagined a variety of methods of
" ciphering with letters." He thought that perhaps A added to B made C ; and B added to
C made D ; and so on ; but there seemed to
him no use in all this. At length he begged
his brother to obtain for him the book. The
schoolmaster readily lent it ; and it is said that

the boy did not sleep that night. He was so delighted with reading about this method, or algebra, as it is called, that he found it impossible to sleep. He afterwards talked with an old English sailor, who happened to know something about the subject, and received some little instruction from him. This person afterwards went to his own country; but, just before he left Salem, he patted Nathaniel upon the head, and said, " Nat, my boy, go on studying as you do now, and you will be a great man one of these days." You will see, before finishing this story, that the prophecy of the old sailor was amply fulfilled.

But all this labor, this constant exertion, must, you will think, have given him friends. Your suspicion is very correct. He became known as a young man of great promise; as one more capable than his elders were of deciding many questions, particularly all those in which any calculations were to be made. Consequently, when about seventeen or eighteen years old, he was frequently called upon, by men much older than himself, to decide important questions. All these he attended to so willingly, that those who applied to him became

2

very much attached to him. But he gained the
notice not merely of common persons, less
learned than himself; but his industry, his fidel-
ity to his employers, his talents, attracted the
notice of men well known in the community.
Among these were two clergymen of the town.
At the church of one of these he attended for
divine worship; and Dr. Bentley used never to
pass the store, without stepping in, to talk with
his young friend. Nathaniel likewise availed
himself of the learning of Dr. Bentley; and
often visited his room, in order to converse with
him. Dr. Prince was the other clergyman.
This gentleman had studied much the same subjects that the apprentice was pursuing, and he
was very glad to see a young man zealous in the
same pursuits. There was another individual,
who kept an apothecary's shop; and it was he,
who, with the aid of the two clergymen, opened
to our young student the means of continuing his
favorite studies, with more success than he had
ever anticipated. Mr. Reed, for that was his
name, likewise gave him permission to use all his
books, of which he had a great many. But the
chief means of study, to which I allude, was the
permission to take books from a library which had

been formed by a number of gentlemen of the town. The kindness of the proprietors of this library was never forgotten by the young apprentice ; and in his will, made fifty years afterwards, he left a thousand dollars, in order to repay the debt of gratitude which he felt he had incurred. But you may want to know something about the formation of this library, and the books of which it was composed. Sometime during the Revolutionary War, alluded to in Chapter I., Dr. Kirwan, an Irishman and a learned man, put the greater part of his library on board a ship, in order to have it carried across the Irish Channel. While on the voyage, the vessel was taken by an American ship of war, and the books were all carried into Beverly, and were afterwards sold at auction, in Salem. Of all in the world these books were perhaps those most needed by the apprentice. He had been studying those sciences chiefly, concerning which there were very few works printed in America ; and suddenly he found himself allowed free access to all the important books which had been printed in Europe, upon these same subjects. You may readily imagine how eagerly he availed himself of the opportunity thus afforded him. Every

two or three days he was seen with a number
of volumes under his arm, going homeward, and
on his arrival there, he read and copied all he
wanted to study at that time or refer to afterwards. He made, in this way, a very large collection of manuscripts, and which now form a part
of his library. Thus, by his own exertions, he,
at the early age of eighteen, became acquainted
with the writings of most of the learned men
of Europe; and he did this, at the time when
he was engaged almost constansly in his store,
for he made it a strict rule, never to allow any
study or reading, however interesting, to inter-
fere with his duties to his employers.

Upon one occasion indeed, a customer called
and purchased a pair of hinges at a time when
the young clerk was deeply engaged in solving
a problem in mathematics, which he thought he
would finish before charging the delivery of them
upon the books, and when the problem was
solved he forgot the matter altogether. In a
few days, the customer called again to pay for
them, when Mr. Hodges himself was in the
shop. The books were examined and gave no
account of this purchase. The clerk upon being applied to, at once recollected the circum-

stance, and the reason of his own forgetfulness, and from that day he made it an invariable rule to finish every matter of business that he began, before undertaking any thing else. Perhaps some of you may remember the story, and when you think of leaving anything half finished, you may repeat to yourselves, "Charge your hinges, and finish what you begin."

Having been instructed in the elements of algebra, Nathaniel soon found that there were books written upon it in other languages, which he knew he ought to read, if he intended to learn as much about it as he could. One of these books was written in a tongue which is known by the name of a dead language, in consequence of its having ceased to be spoken by the people of the country in which it was originally used. It was in Latin. This language usually requires many years of study, if one wishes to read it well, even when he has able instructers. Our hero, however, never thought of the difficulties he had to surmount, but commenced, alone, the study of it, June 1790. He was soon in trouble. He could not understand his Latin book on mathematics. He asked many who had been at college, but they were puzzled by the peculiar expressions as much as he was. At length, however, by the aid of his friend, Dr. Bentley, and afterwards, of a German who gave him lessons, he succeeded in mastering the greatest work in modern times, written by Sir Isaac Newton, who, you know, was one of the most renowned philosophers that has ever lived in this world. He moreover discovered in one part of it, a mistake, which, several years afterwards, he published ; but he was deterred from doing so at first, because a very much older person than he, a professor in the college, said that the apprentice was mistaken.

But Latin was not the only language that he learned. Finding in the Kirwan library many books upon mathematics, written in French, he determined to learn that tongue, likewise. Accordingly, at the age of nineteen, (May 15, 1792,) he began to study it. Fortunately, he was able to make an arrangement with the above-mentioned foreigner, who wished to learn English. Mr. Jordy agreed to teach the apprentice French, on condition that Nathaniel would teach him English. For sixteen months they met regularly, a certain number of times a week, and the consequences were very important to the youth's future success in life. One circumstance took place during this study of French which I think it important to mention. Nathaniel, thinking merely to learn to *read* a French book, supposed that it would be scarcely necessary to spend time in learning accurately to *pronounce* the words. These, as is the case in the English tongue, are frequently pronounced very differently from the manner in which we should be led to speak them, if we judged merely from their mode of being spelled. His master protested against teaching, without reference to the pronunciation; and, after much arguing, Nathaniel consented to the wishes of his instructer, and he studied the language in such a way, that he could converse with a Frenchman, as well as read a French book. You will soon see the good that resulted. But now I must close my chapter.

CHAPTER III.

THOUGH so interested in his studies, Nathaniel tried, as we have seen, never to neglect
a known duty. Though busily engaged, whenever any one came to the store he was ready to
leave study, in order to attend to him. And he
did this so cheerfully, and with so bright a smile,
that all were pleased to meet him. His young
companions loved him, for he was not one of
those vain persons who think themselves more
important than others, because they are more
learned. On the contrary, what he knew himself he longed to impart to others. He was a
member of a juvenile club, for the discussion of
different subjects. In this association his opinion
had much weight, because he rarely spoke, and

never, unless he had something of importance
to say.

Some of his comrades were very fond of music.
He had originally a great taste for it. Music, at
that time, was less cultivated than it is now ; and
generally, those who practised it were fond of
drinking ardent spirits. Nathaniel's love of the
flute led him, at times, to meet with several
young men of this class. In fact, he was so
much delighted with their company, that he began to forget his studies. Day after day, he spent
his leisure hours in their society ; and, for a time,
all else was neglected. At length, he began to
think thus : " What am I doing ? forgetting my
studies, in order to be with young men whose
only recommendation is, that they love music ?
Their characters I despise, though I love their
songs. I will do so no longer." He decided,
and immediately he forsook them.

May every boy who reads this remember it,
and try, if ever led into temptation as the apprentice was, to say, " I will not," with the
same determined courage that he did.

The time was fast approaching, when he was
about to leave the business of shop-keeping, and
enter upon the more active duties of life. It is

true, that, to a certain extent, he had been engaged in active life ever since entering his apprenticeship. At the age of ten, he had left the home of his loved mother, and had been obliged to depend much upon himself. His father's habits had wholly prevented him from being of service to the family. The mother had died; the family had been broken up; and Nathaniel had thus at an early age been thrown upon the world. After having remained with Ropes & Hodges until they gave up business, Nathaniel entered the shop of Samuel C. Ward, which was a similar establishment, and there he remained until he was twenty-one years old. He then quitted, forever, this employment.

In 1794, by a law of the State, every town was obliged to have an accurate survey and measurement made of its limits. Captain Gibaut and Dr. Bentley were appointed to superintend this business, by the Selectmen of Salem. Believing that the calculating powers of the apprentice would be useful to them, he was made assistant; and, during the summer of 1794, he was thus occupied. Thus we see how his studies already began to be useful to him. For his share of the pay, on this occasion, he received one hundred and thirty-five dollars. Towards the termination of the summer, Mr. Derby, a rich ship-owner in Salem, wished Capt. Gibaut to take command of a vessel to Cadiz, and thence round the Cape of Good Hope to the East Indies. Captain G. consented, and he proposed to Mr. Bowditch to go with him, as clerk. Mr. B. agreed to the terms, and arrangements were made, when, owing to some difficulty with Mr. Derby, Captain Gibaut resigned to Captain H. Prince. Mr. Bowditch was unknown to the latter; but, at the suggestion of Mr. Derby, who had heard of the talents and industry of the clerk, the same arrangements were continued by Captain Prince.

Thus we see a new era in his life was beginning; and let us look a moment at him. He is now twenty-one years of age. More learned, already, than many much older than himself, in consequence of his untiring industry, and his devotion to duty. Yet he is modest and retiring. He is still full of joyousness and fun, at times, and always ready for acts of kindness. Above all, he is a good youth; no immorality has ever stained him; he is as pure as snow. His love of truth had been given him by his mother;

and, since her death, he has loved it still more.
It is to him a bright light, as it were, to guide
him.   Cannot we foresee his career ?

On January 11, 1795, that is, when he was
a few months more than twenty-one years of
age, he sailed from Salem, in the ship Henry.
Though he went as clerk, he was prepared to
undertake the more active duties of sailor and
mate of the vessel.   Thinking that he should
be too much occupied to be able to read, he
took very few books ; and therefore he devoted
much more time to observations of the heavenly
bodies, the state of the weather, &c., while at
sea, and upon the manners and habits of the
nations he visited, than he did to reading.
Though he had not been educated as a sailor-
boy, his studies had prepared him to understand
the most important part of a seaman's life, the
art of guiding the vessel from one shore to
another, across the ocean.   In other words, he
had studied much on navigation, and copied
books upon that subject.

The journal which he kept during the voyage
is quite long.   One of the first lines you meet,
on opening the book, is the motto which he
chose for himself.   It is in Latin, and means,

that *he would do what he thought to be right, and not obey the dictates of any man.* He notes the events of every day, most of which are similar ; but occasionally, something unusual occurs.

February 7, 1795, he writes thus: " At 10, A. M., spoke a ship, twenty-five days out from Liverpool, bound to Africa. We discovered her this morning, just before sunrise, and supposed her to be a frigate." They discovered, soon, that it was a negro slave-ship, and he exclaims thus: " God grant that the detestable traffic which she pursues may soon cease, and that the tawny sons of Africa may be permitted quietly to enjoy the blessings of liberty, in their native land."

" February 22. We remember with gratitude that this is the anniversary of the birth of our beloved Washington, the man who unites all hearts. May he long continue a blessing to his country and to mankind at large ! "

During the passage to the Isle of Bourbon, situated, as you know, east of the southern extremity of Africa, he frequently alludes to his native land, in terms of respect and love. On May 8th, the ship arrived in the harbor of Bourbon. Perhaps you may like to see his description of the town.

" May 9th. After dinner, Captain P., Mr. B., and I, went to see the town. It is a fine place. All the streets run in straight lines from the shore, and cross one another at right angles. There is a church here, with a priest to officiate. I went into it. We afterwards went into the republican garden. It is a beautiful place, though at present much neglected. The different walks are made to meet in the centre, and form the figure of a star, each one of the rays of which is formed by thirty-four mango trees, placed from twelve to fourteen feet apart. All the houses of the island are built very low ; they have no chimneys. They are two stories high, (about ten feet), have lattice windows, outside of which are wooden ones to keep off the sun and rain. The floors are made of the wood of the country, on which they rub wax, as the women of America do on their furniture. It makes them very slippery."—There are other places, of which he speaks, and in them he finds flower-gardens, in abundance, intermixed with groves of coffee and orange trees, &c.

He afterwards alludes to the poor slaves, who,
it appeared, suffered as much there as they do
in some other places, at the present day.

He visits the people of the place, and finds
them superstitious and vicious. Alluding to the
vice, he found there, he writes : " I was reminded of the beautiful words of Solomon, in the
Proverbs."—This was not the only occasion on
which he remembered his Bible ; and it seemed
to have a kindly influence over him, always. On
one occasion, several young men argued with
him about its truth ; and, having heard them
patiently, he at length struck his breast : " Talk
no more about it. I know that the Bible is
true ; that it is capable of doing to me the
greatest good. I know so, by the feelings I
have here."

After remaining in this corrupt place until
July 25, he set sail for home, and arrived in
Salem, January 11, 1796, having been absent
exactly twelve months.

CHAPTER IV.

[*From* 1796 *to* 1797, — *aged* 23 — 4.]

Second Voyage. — Visits Lisbon. — Island of Madeira :
festival and games there. — Anecdotes of his skill as an
accountant. — Doubles Cape of Good Hope. — Albatrosses. — Arrival at Manilla. — Extracts from Journal.
Curious boat. — Earthquake. — Voyage home.

AFTER remaining at home about two
months, he again sailed in the same ship and
with Captain Prince. On the twenty-sixth of
the following March, they got under weigh
from Salem harbor ; but, being prevented, by
the severity of the wind, from getting out of the
bay, the anchor was dropped during the night,
and on the ensuing morning, under fair but
strong breezes, our hero was again on his way
across the wide Atlantic. His course was towards Lisbon, situated at the mouth of the river
Tagus, in Portugal. The first part of the voyage was unpleasant, because cloudy and stormy
weather prevailed most of the time ; but during
the latter part, under pleasant and mild breezes
from the south, the ship rode gaily onwards,
and, on the morning of April 24th, the sailor

discovered the rock of Lisbon, with its beautiful
and romantic country behind it. Lisbon is the
chief city of Portugal, and presents a very
superb appearance from a vessel which is entering the harbor. It is the principal commercial
place for the kingdom; therefore, its inhabitants
are among the richest. In consequence of its
being the place of residence of the kings of
Portugal, many magnificent country-seats, or
villas, are seen on all the vine-covered hills of
the adjacent country.

The stay at this city was but short, and the
opportunities for visiting the interesting places
in it, very limited. Mr. Bowditch seems not to
have been particularly pleased with its appearance. At the time he was there, probably
much less attention was paid to the cleanliness
of the streets, than there is now. But he spent
the twenty-eighth and twenty-ninth of April in
walking about the city, and says, in his Journal,
that he "found nothing remarkable."

It was at Lisbon that Mr. Bowditch discovered the advantage of having learned to speak
French, to which I alluded at the close of the
second chapter. Though a Portuguese port,
the custom-house officers understood French,

3

and no one on board but he could speak any
other language than the English. The consequence was, that he acted as interpreter, and
was, of course, of incalculable advantage. This
incident made a deep impression upon his mind ;
and in after-life, when any doubted about the
importance of any kind of knowledge, because,
for the time, it seemed useless, he would reply,
" Oh, study every thing, and your learning will,
some time, be of service. I once said that I
would not learn to *speak* French, because I
thought that I should never leave my native
town ; yet, within a few years afterwards, I was
in a foreign port, and I became sole interpreter
of the ship's crew, in consequence of my ability
to speak this language."

On the 30th, having taken on board a quantity of wine, they were ready again for sea ; but,
owing to bad weather, did not sail until the
sixth of May, when the ship dropped down the
river. On the sixth, it was on its way to the
Island of Madeira, which is a small island, situ-a-
ted about three hundred and sixty miles from the
northern part of Africa. At eleven o'clock,
May 15th, the island was discovered ; and, under full sail, the ship swept along the shore,

until nine in the evening, when they hailed a
pilot, who came on board from the town of
Funchal. Mr. Pintard, the American Consul
of the place, greeted them very cordially. He
spent six days there, taking in more wine, for
which the country is famous, and sailed from it
on Thursday morning, May 26th, 1796. During this residence at Mr. Pintard's, he saw some
feats of horsemanship, about which you may like
to hear. They are thus described in his Journal: " A ring being suspended by a small wire
about ten feet from the ground, at the entrance
of the gate of the public garden, a horseman
attempted to strike it, and carry it off while
upon full gallop. If he gained the prize, he was
attended by the master of ceremonies, mounted on a small colt fantastically adorned with
ribands, &c., with a most deformed mask, who
generally gave him a reward fully proportioned
to the merit of the action, perhaps a whistle, a
small flower, or some little image." During the
next day, no business was done by the inhabitants, but the whole of it was devoted to amusements similar to those of the preceding. Again,
there were masquerades, and some of the richest
men in the place joined with the crowd, masked

like the people.   Others were very richly
dressed, like Turks, East Indians, &c.   One of
them wore a head-dress, worth, it was said, forty
or fifty thousand dollars."   From this description, slight as it is, we may see the difference in
the customs between these inhabitants of Madeira and the Americans.

Captain Prince relates the following anecdotes, which occurred during their residence at
Madeira.   I shall use Capt. Prince's words:

"I was one day walking with an American
shipmaster at Madeira, who, in the course of
conversation, asked me who that young man
(alluding to Mr. Bowditch) was.   I replied,
that he was clerk of the ship under my command, and remarked, that he was a great calcu-
lator.   "Well," said the gentleman, " I can set
him a sum that he can't do."   I merely answered that I did not believe it.   The gentleman then proposed a wager of a dinner to all
the American masters in port, that he could set
him such a sum.   The wager was accepted by
me, and we repaired to the hotel, where we
found Mr. B. alone.   The gentleman was introduced, and the question stated to Mr. Bowditch,
with the interrogatory, can you do it ?   The re-

ply was, yes. The great sum, which had puzzled the brains of the gentleman and all his
friends at home, for a whole winter, was done in
a few minutes. I remember the sum (as it was
called) to have been this : To dig a ditch round
an acre of land, how deep and how wide must
that ditch be, to raise the acre of land one foot ?

" One day, Mr. Bowditch and myself received a visit from a Mr. Murray, a Scotchman,
who was at that port, having under his charge a
valuable cargo of English goods, and who made
many inquiries concerning the Americans. He
asked particularly, what passage we came
against the northeast monsoon, and remarked,
that it was very surprising that the Americans
should come so far and undertake such difficult
voyages with so little knowledge as they possessed of the science of navigation. In reply to
his remark, I told him, that I had on board
twelve men, all of whom were as well acquainted with working lunar observations, for all the
practical purposes of navigation, as Sir Isaac
Newton would be, should he come on earth.
Mr. M. asked how my crew came by that
knowledge. I told him, in the same manner
that other men came by theirs. He thought it

so wonderful, that (as he afterwards told me) he went down to the landing place on Sunday, to see my *knowing* crew come on shore. During all this conversation, Mr. Bowditch remained silent, sitting with his slate pencil in his mouth, and as modest as a maid. Mr. Kean, a broker, who was also present, observed to Murray, ' Sir, if you knew what I know concerning that ship, you would not talk quite so fast.' ' And what do you know?' asked Murray. ' I know,' replied Kean, ' that there is more knowledge of navigation on board that American ship, (the Astrea,) than there ever was in all the ships that ever came into Manilla Bay.' "

May 26th, as we have already said, he sailed for India. On July 1st, the island of Trinidad hove in sight. They did not stop there, but, keeping on their course steadily, two days afterwards crossed the Tropic of Capricorn, in the Southern Hemisphere. On the 17th, during the night, it having rained during the day, the young sailor observed wna we rarely see in this part of the world and on land, but which is not uncommon at sea, a beautiful lunar rainbow. It is caused in the same manner as those rainbows which are seen after a summer shower, when

the sun is just coming forth again in glory, and
the clouds, which cause the bow to be formed,
are passing away afar off in the opposite part of
the heavens. But the difference between the
solar and lunar rainbows, is like that which
exists between greatness and gentleness. We
admire and wonder at the sight of the bow of
Jehovah in the cloud by day, but we love to
look upon the mild and peaceful Lunar Iris,
because all its tints are so rich, and delicately
beautiful.

August 1st, the Journal says : " All the latter
part of these twenty-four hours fine breezes and
pleasant, smooth sea. Ever since crossing the
Cape, [of Good Hope,] we have seen a great
number of Albatrosses, but no fish." These
birds are the largest of marine birds. They at
times fly and swim, (for they are web-footed,)
to a great distance from land, living upon the
fish and other things which may fall in their way.
It is said that, as they come gently rising over
the waves of the sea, they present a very pleasing sight to the mariner who has been for many
months separated from living things, upon the
wide ocean.

For some weeks afterwards, the ship met with

severe weather, until September 7th, when, according to previous expectation, they perceived
the land of the island of Java ; but the day before their arrival at that place, a curious phenomenon was observed, the account of which I
will copy from the Journal. "At 7, P. M., the
water, as for the two nights past, became of a
perfect milk color, through the whole extent of
the horizon. We drew a bucket of it, in order
to determine whether there was any thing in it,
to account for the curious phenomenon. When
seen by candlelight, nothing could be observed ;
but, when carried into a dark place, it appeared
full of small bright cylindric substances, of the
nature of a jelly, about the size of a small wire,
and a quarter of an inch long. Some large jel-
lies floated on the water at the same time, and
looked like long pieces of wood. The sky all
this time was perfectly clear ; not a cloud to be
seen. About 3, A. M., the water began to take
its usual color. Next morning, we examined
the water which had appeared so shining in the
night, but nothing could be discovered in it,
although it was viewed in a very dark place.
In the forenoon, the sea appeared somewhat col-
ored, of a greenish hue, but some of it being

taken up, and carried from the light, appeared colorless."

The next morning the highlands of the island of Java come in sight, on the horizon, at the distance of about twenty miles towards the east. The Journal of the passage through the Straits of Sunda is interesting, because the greatest care was necessary to keep the ship off from the shoals which abound there. Moreover, the current runs at times very swiftly here, the Strait being between the large islands of Sumatra and Java. On the 9th, the force of this current, and strong head winds, caused the captain to cast anchor two or three times. Finally, on the 17th, the ship was fairly out of the Straits of Sunda and Straits of Banca, having been ten days, during sultry weather, toiling, with much danger, amid coral reef and shoals. The remainder of the voyage, along by the coast of Borneo to the city of Manilla, the capital of the chief of the Philippine islands, was more speedy; and, at six in the morning of Sunday, Oct. 2nd, 1796, the island of Luzor hove in sight towards the east, about eighteen miles; and that same evening they cast anchor in Manilla Bay; it being a little more

than six months since the sailor had left his home
in Salem.

The following are some extracts from his journal, while in the city. Under date of October
4th, he says : " No coffee can be procured here;
the Spaniards, not being very fond of it, culti-
vate the cocoa, instead. The common drink of
the natives are sweatmeats and water, which
they say is wholesome and agreeable. Large
quantities of wax are produced here, but it is
very dear, owing to the vast consumption of it
in the churches, of which there are a great
number in Manilla and its environs. There are
a few bishops in the island, and one archbishop,
whose power is very great. The priests are
very powerful, every native wearing the image
of the Virgin Mary, a cross, or some such thing.
No books are allowed to be imported here contrary to their religion. The commandant who
makes the visit examines every vessel. * * *
The inhabitants of the city and suburbs are very
numerous, amounting to nearly three hundred
thousand. In the Philippines, there are about
two or three millions. A great number are
Chinese ; and in general, they are a well-made

people. Their common dress is a shirt and
trowsers, or jackets and trowsers. The women
have great numbers of handkerchiefs about them,
so as to be entirely covered. The natives are
well used by the Spaniards ; the king of Spain,
in all his public papers, calling them his children." From these extracts you may judge of
young Bowditch's mode of studying a people
when residing with strangers. He afterwards
speaks of their games, &c.

The following description of a boat appears
on record of October 5th : " At twelve, set sail
for Cavite in one of the passage-boats, which is
very inconvenient for passengers ; being nearly
three hours before arriving at Cavite, during
which time I was basking in the sun. Their
boats and manner of sailing are very curious.
Having generally light winds, they make their
mat sails very large, and the boats, made of the
bodies of trees, are very long and narrow, so
that there would be great danger of upsetting,
if it were not for " out-riggers " which they
have on each side, consisting of two bamboos
about eight or ten feet long, whose ends
are joined to another long bamboo, running
lengthwise of the boat. The lee one, on a flaw

of wind, sinks a little in the water, and, being
buoyant, keeps the boats from upsetting, and, on
the weather (that is, towards the wind) ones,
the persons in the boat are continually going out
and in, according to the force of the breeze. In
a fresh breeze, there will be six or eight at the
end of the bamboo, there being ropes leading
from the top of the mast to different parts of
the bamboo, to support them as they go. By
this means, they keep the boat always upright,
and make it sail very fast, in a good breeze,
going five or six knots." After this, a good
account is given of the mode of counting, used
by the Malays.

"Nov. 5. About two, P. M., there came
on, without any preceding noise, a very violent
shock of an earthquake. It commenced toward
the north, and run very nearly in a southerly
direction. It continued nearly two minutes;
every thing appeared in motion. When it happened, the captain and myself were sitting, reading, and we immediately ran out of the house.
All the natives were down on their knees, in
the middle of the streets, praying and crossing
themselves. It was the most violent earthquake
known for a number of years. It threw down

a large house about half a league from the city, untiled one of their churches, and did considerable damage to the houses about the city and its suburbs. Nothing of it was felt on board the shipping."

On Monday, December 12th, having sold their wines and laden their vessel with sugar, indigo, pepper, and hides, the party set sail from Manilla, heartily tired with the vices and superstitions of the place. Retracing their course through the Straits of Sunda, with much difficulty they regained the Indian Ocean, and then, setting full sail, they once more looked towards home.

In coming round the Cape of Good Hope, the wind was peculiarly favorable. During their passage, several ships were met with, all of whom told them of home, and of the beginning of troubles between America and France, and England. Finally, at six, A. M., saw Cape Ann towards the northwest, and at two, P. M., May 22, 1797, the vessel was riding at anchor in Salem harbor, having been about half round the world, and nearly fourteen months from Salem.

CHAPTER V.

[*From* 1797 *to* 1800, — *aged* 24 — 7.]

Marriage. — Third voyage; visits Spain. — Dangers. — Earl St. Vincent's fleet. — Arrival at Cadiz. — Observatory at Cadiz. — Sails for Alicant. — Passage through the Straits of Gibraltar. — Privateers: chased by one: anecdotes of Mr. B's love of study shown then. — Hears news of the death of his wife: consoles himself with mathematical studies. — More troubles with privateers. — Leaves Alicant. — Advantages derived from his visit to Spain. — Fourth voyage; to India. — Extracts from Journal on viewing a ship that was engaged in the slave-trade. — Arrival at Java: introduction to the Governor: respect formerly paid to him. — Anecdote of English Navy Officers. — Goes to Batavia and Manilla. — Observations of Jupiter while becalmed near the Celebean Islands. — Voyage home.

DURING these two voyages, Mr. Bowditch had been engaged in trade for himself, and having thereby gained a small fortune, he wished to remain at home, and enjoy the blessings of domestic life, from which he had been separated at the age of ten years, when he left the abode of his parents. In accordance with this wish, on the twenty-fifth day of March, 1798, he married a very excellent and intelligent woman, named Elizabeth Boardman. But in a few

months, he was again called to a seafaring life.
His young and beautiful wife was already beginning to show symptoms of that disease which
eventually removed her from her husband and
friends. It was a hard struggle for the ten-
derly attached couple to separate themselves ;
but duty called the husband, and obedience to
duty was always his watchword. Accordingly,
by August 15th, 1798, he was prepared for sea,
in the same ship, with the same owner, Captain
Derby, and his friend Captain Prince. On this
occasion he went as joint supercargo. It was on
the twenty-first of August ; nearly five months
from the date of his marriage ; that he bade
adieu to his wife. He never saw her more.
Full of devotedness to him, she however urged
him to go forward in the performance of the
right, unconscious that she should never more
embrace him. During his absence she died, at
the early age of eighteen years.

One of the objects of the present voyage was,
to go to Cadiz, the chief southern port in Spain.
It was rather dangerous, at this time, for any
vessel to sail towards Europe, as the Revolution
in France had taken place only a short time
before, and Europe was beginning to rise against

that country ; and as Spain, at that period, was
united with France, an English fleet was hover-
ing about the Straits of Gibraltar. The consequence was, that it was of great importance to
avoid all vessels, for fear of meeting a privateer.

On the nineteenth of September, after nearly
a month's voyage, they came within sight of the
shores of Spain ; and at seven, A. M., the next
day, they discovered the English fleet, under
command of Earl St. Vincent, several leagues
to the eastward of them. On this same day
they were boarded by the captain of an American vessel, who informed them that the privateers were very numerous in the Straits.

By Mr. Bowditch's Journal, we learn the
following :

" On Thursday afternoon, twentieth of September, the winds continued light and variable
to the westward. Captain Prince steered di-
rectly for Earl St. Vincent's fleet, and at two,
P. M., the Hector, of seventy-four guns, Capt.
Camel, sent his lieutenant on board, ordering
us to bear down to him. Captain Prince went
aboard, was treated politely, and received a
passport to enter Cadiz." On the twenty-first,
at four, P. M., anchor was cast in that harbor.

The state in which poor Spain was, at this time, was miserable enough. There was but one newspaper in the whole kingdom, and that was printed at Madrid. Every thing was degraded about that once noble and brave-hearted people. Upon the appearance of Cadiz, the Journal says thus: " The streets of the city, although narrow, are very neatly paved, and swept every day, so that they are very clean. They have broad, flat stones at the sides. All the houses are of stone, with roofs but little sloping. There are fortifications all around the city."

" September 29th, 1798. This day, news came of the destruction of the French fleet, in the Mediterranean Sea, by Lord Nelson." Of this event you will read in history, at some future time; but it was deemed very important at that time by the whole world. It was one of the most formidable checks received by the French, after they had begun to overrun Europe.

This news, of course, was deeply interesting to our voyager; but, although excited by the political and military contests of the day, he did not forget the subject to which from earliest years he had devoted himself. You will per-

4

ceive, from the following extracts from his Journal, that he now was studying astronomy. In fact, he had been reading, during his previous voyages, many of the greatest works on mathematics and astronomy.

"November 12th. During our residence in Cadiz we formed an acquaintance with Count Mallevante, who, before the Revolution, commanded a French frigate at Martinico, and at present is a post-captain in the Spanish navy. He carried us to the New Observatory, built on the island of Cadiz, where we were shown all the instruments they had mounted. There were not any of them very new. The person who went with us was named Cosmo de Churruca. I promised to send him, on my arrival in America, the works of Dr. Holyoke, on Meteorology. I gave him my method of working a lunar observation, which he was to print at the end of the Nautical Almanac."

"At half past four, P. M., got under way, and beat out of the harbor of Cadiz, in company with three other American vessels ; which sailed under the protection of the Astrea." They were destined for Alicant, and consequently their course lay through the Straits of

Gibraltar, up along the south-eastern coast of Spain. On the afternoon of the fourteenth, they fell in again with the English fleet, which, with those under their convoy, consisted of forty-five vessels. As the fleet was steering in the same direction, they kept company with it, being all bound for the Straits of Gibraltar. On next day, saw another convoy, of twenty vessels, and two of those accompanying the Astrea joined it. The Astrea was obliged to fall behind, because the remaining vessel under its protection sailed too slowly. On the eighteenth, the whole convoy entered the Straits, except one, which was chased by French privateers, ten of which could be counted in full view; but, on the approach of the Astrea, the enemy retreated.

The moon was shining brightly, on the night of the nineteenth of November, 1799. Many times had the bell broken over the silent sea from the ship's deck, telling of the passing hours; when, suddenly, the crew of the Astrea was called to quarters, for a suspicious sail was seen bearing down towards them. The cannon, of which nineteen were on board, were all cleared for action, and every man, placed at his post, watched anxiously as the privateer came

rapidly towards them. Captain Prince assigned
to Mr. Bowditch a station in the cabin, through
whcih the powder was to be passed to the deck.
When all on deck was ready, and that deep
and solemn silence which always pervades every
part of a ship that is just approaching the
enemy, was beginning to creep over those on
board the Astrea, the Captain stepped for a
moment into the cabin, to see if every thing was
in order, and " there sat Mr. Bowditch at the
cabin table, with his slate and pencil in hand,
and with the cartridges lying by his side."
Entirely absorbed with his problem, he forgot
all danger, thus showing that his love of science,
even when in imminent peril, was superior to all
feelings of fear. This anecdote, doubtless, will
amuse you, and it reminds me of the geometri-
cian Archimedes, who lived two hundred years
before Christ, who, as some of you may know,
was slain by the soldiers of the Roman General
Marcellus, when they sacked the city of Syra-
cuse. Archimedes had labored much for his
countrymen, during the siege, but finally became so engaged in his studies, that he was
totally ignorant that the soldiers had taken pos-
session of the town, until they attacked and

killed him. Fortunately, in the case of Mr. Bowditch, no evil ensued. Captain Prince himself could not restrain his feelings, but burst into a loud laugh, and asked Mr. Bowditch whether he could make his will at that moment, to which question Mr. B. answered, with a smile, in the affirmative. Captain Prince adds, " But on all occasions of danger, he manifested great firmness, and, after the affair of the privateer, (which, by the by, did not molest us,) he requested to be stationed at one of the guns, which request was granted him."

In this way, they continued cruising along the beautiful Mediterranean, but perpetually exposed to danger. Now, they come within sight of the high lands of Malaga, and shortly they fly away from some pirate on the broad sea. Now, they are quietly sailing along under the warm and sunny skies of an Andalusian climate ; and again, in the course of a few hours, are driven by the current and tempest far away, to the southwest. Finally, after a tedious passage, the ship was moored, on Friday evening, November twenty-third, in the harbor of Alicant. After considerable difficulty, on account of the city authorities, for fear of disease being brought

into the place, by the crews of the ships, they
were at length allowed to go on shore.   But
melancholy tidings awaited our voyager.   By a
Salem vessel that had arrived at Cadiz, news
came of the death of his wife, sometime in the
preceding October.   He made no complaints
however.   He never thought it right to complain of the trials that fell upon him, but he
quietly sought to interest his mind in his favorite
pursuit of astronomy.   He always did so, whenever any trouble came upon him.   In this way
he consoled himself, and was not a burden to
others, by being of a discontented spirit.

January 24th, 1799, having finished loading
their ship with brandy, they would have sailed,
had not the wind prevented.   On February
eleventh, they were still detained by head-winds,
but now, to their discomfort, they saw a French
privateer cruising off in the bay at the mouth of
the harbor.   It was evidently waiting to entrap
some one of the American vessels.   On the
next day, the daring of the privateer commander arose to such a height, that he rowed in his
barge all around the American fleet, and insult-
ed some of the people.   Towards evening of
February thirteenth, Mr. Bowditch narrowly

escaped serious difficulty with them, as the privateer barge and the American boat, coming from shore, came in contact; but the former received the most damage, and Mr. Bowditch got safely on board the Astrea. On the fourteenth, the brigand of the sea departed, and his ship was soon seen gradually losing itself in the distance over the blue Mediterranean.

On the next day, the convoy sailed. It consisted of five vessels, and, by twenty-four hours of favorable breezes, they were brought within thirty miles of the coast of Barbary; and, after some trouble, in consequence of being obliged to take in tow those of the convoy which sailed more slowly, the Astrea was fairly out from the Straits of Gibraltar by February twenty-fourth, that is, three days from the time of leaving Alicant.

During half the passage home, some of the convoy were in company with them. They had rough seas; but, on the sixth of April, at ten o'clock at night, Mr. Bowditch arrived in Salem habor, having been absent nearly nine months.

This visit to Spain was of service to him, in many respects. He there obtained many books

on astronomy and navigation, and some celebrated works on history, all of which he studied
with care, on his voyage home. He, moreover,
had gained some knowledge by his visit to the
observatory.

He was not destined to remain at home a long
while; but the Astrea having been sold to a
merchant in Boston, Mr. Bowditch sailed
with Captain Prince from that city, on the
twenty-third of the following July, bound for
India. It was a long, and, to most persons, a
tedious, voyage that he was about to undertake;
but to Mr. Bowditch it was the means of improvement. While the ship was sailing quietly along, or sinking lazily from one swell of the
sea to another, or borne towards heaven on the
most violent gale, Mr. Bowditch was still laboring at his books. During this voyage, as during
the preceding, he did not perform much duty,
except when in port; and consequently, on
board ship, he had a great deal of time to be
devoted to study. And he worthily filled every
moment with reading and intense study, to improve himself or others. Very few incidents
worth mentioning occurred during the voyage;
but, on the fifteenth of September, 1799, we

find the following in his Journal: " The ship, in sight yesterday, soon proved to be an English Guineaman. As we came up with him, he fired a gun to leward, which we returned. As we came nearer, he fired one to windward. We returned the compliment, and nearly hulled him. When within hail, he ordered our boat out, which Captain Prince refused, telling him to come on board, if he wanted any thing. Finally, he requested Captain P. to haul out our boat, as his was caulking, which we could plainly see. Mr. Carlton went on board with the clearance, and the surgeon came aboard of us, and, after examining our papers and acting in a manner becoming a Guineaman, they made sail."

In order to understand this allusion to the Guineaman, you should know, that, at the time we are reading of, the greater part of English merchants, especially those of Liverpool, were engaged in the horrid traffic called the Slave Trade. Immense numbers of vessels were annually sent from Liverpool, and other places in England, for the sole purpose of sailing to the coast of Africa, there to get a cargo of the poor natives, whom they carried to the West-Indian Islands and America, in order that they might be sold, as slaves, into perpetual bondage. Men, women, and children, were taken indiscriminately, and crammed together, like bales of cotton or any other goods, between the decks of the vessels. You may imagine, that those who could engage in such abominable proceedings must have lost all the feelings of humanity. They were used to blood and rapine; hence you can understand the reason why Mr. Bowditch uses the term of reproach that he does. I thank heaven, and I feel sure that you will agree with me, that, by the efforts of devoted men and women in England and elsewhere, that trade has been formally abolished by Great Britain; and that every man who now sets his foot on British soil becomes free. We will hope that the same beautiful truth may ere long be proclaimed through our country, in which, as you know, there are now three millions of slaves. But, to return to the Astrea.

On December 17th, they arrived at Batavia, the chief city of the island of Java. The following will give you some idea of the place and persons in it.

" Upon our first arrival, after making our report to the customhouse, we proceeded to the Saabandar, who introduced us to the Governor and the Governor-General, who is Commander-in-chief, and formerly lived in all the splendor of an Asiatic monarch. At present, the outward marks of respect are far less than they were twenty or thirty years ago. In former times, he was attended by his guards, preceded by two trumpeters. Every carriage was forced to stop, and the persons within obliged to dismount, under the penalty of one hundred ducatoons, (about $167.) Captain ———— refused even to stop his carriage, and forced his coachman to drive on. The officers of an English squadron, lying at Batavia, in order to show their contempt of the procession, formed a party similar to that attending the Governor, only, instead of the aids with their staves, one of the officers bore a staff with a cow's horn tipped with gold, and another an empty bottle. The rest of the officers of the fleet met this procession, and made their respects to it, as the natives did to the Governor. At present, all these practices are brought into contempt, so that none now stop for any officers of government."

The Astrea remained but four days at Batavia, the captain finding that he could not fill his

vessel with coffee, as he intended. Consequently, after taking a fresh supply of provisions and
of water, they weighed anchor, and bore towards
the north, with the intention of visiting Manilla,
as on his second voyage. Traversing the Straits
of Macassar, they passed slowly up through the
China Sea, and anchored in Manilla Bay on
the fourteenth of February, 1800. During this
passage, we find Mr. Bowditch still occupied
in the study of science. When floating, becalmed among the islands, amidst the quiet-
ness of night, he is observing the appearance of
the planet Jupiter, and studying the motions of
its beautiful satellites. Doubtless, as he was
thus occupied, he thought of the immense power
of that Being who first placed the bright planet
in its place, and told it to revolve around our
sun, while its own little satellites, like four
moons, were to keep it company, silently and
grandly, in its mysterious course.

After remaining at Manilla long enough to get
a cargo, the ship was prepared for home. On
the twenty-third of March, it sailed ; and, during a passage of six months, very little occurred
to interrupt Mr. Bowditch's daily labors. It
arrived on the sixteenth of September, 1800.
About a fortnight before this, September the

second, a ship was observed to windward, which
bore down upon them. By the captain, they
were informed of the melancholy news (as Mr.
B. says in his Journal) "of the death of our
beloved Washington. Thus," continues he,
" has finished the career of that illustrious man,
that great general, that consummate statesman,
that elegant writer, that real patriot, that friend
to his country and to all mankind ! " This character of Washington is true ; but there is one
point to which Mr. B. makes no allusion, — the
love of truth displayed by that good man, from
his earliest years. It was a character which Mr.
B. must have loved, even if he had not been a
great statesman and patriot ; for Washington
was a just man ; and goodness and love of
truth were always of much more importance, in
Mr. B.'s opinion, than any greatness.

During these different voyages, he gained
more property. Having obtained, likewise,
what was much better, a good report among his
fellow-citizens, as a man of great learning, perseverance, extraordinary skill in the transaction
of business, and unyielding uprightness, he determined to remain at home, and he therefore
bade farewell to the sailor's life, as he supposed,
forever.

CHAPTER VI.

[*From* 1800 *to* 1803, — *aged* 27 — 30.]

Second marriage: character of his wife. — Mr. B. engages
in commerce, for two years. — School committee. —
East-India Marine Society: a description of the annual
meeting of this society. — Mr. B. becomes part owner of
ship Putnam, and sails for India. -- Anecdote, occur-
rence a few days after leaving Salem. — Studies during
the long voyage. — Begins to study and make notes upon
La Place's "Mecanique Celeste."—Arrival off Sumatra:
difficulties there. — Boarded by English man-of-war. —
Revisits Isle of France. — Journal extracts about modes
of procuring pepper: seasons for it, &c. — Incident on
approaching Salem harbor. — Decision of Mr. B.

On the twenty-eighth of October, 1800,
Mr. Bowditch married his cousin, Mary Inger-
soll. She was destined to live with him thirty-
five years, and was the source of much of his
happiness in life. She was a person, in some
respects, as remarkable as her husband. She
was possessed of an extraordinary good judg-
ment, unwearying kindness and love, an elastic
cheerfulness, which scarcely any thing could
subdue, and very strong religious feelings. She
was constantly trying to aid him. Instead of
seeking for enjoyment in display, she preferred

economical retirement and great but respect-
able frugality, in order that her husband might
pursue more thoroughly and easily his favorite
studies, and might purchase books of science.
Instead of collecting beautiful furniture, she
called her visitors to see the rich new works of
learning, that her husband had imported from
foreign lands. Yet, with all this devoted love,
with all this intense reverence for his talents
and virtues, she remained his true friend, and
never shrunk from fully expressing her own
opinion upon every matter of duty ; and if, per-
chance, she differed from him, she maintained
her side of the question with the zeal of a true
saint. It has been often said, that, had Mr.
Bowditch been united with a woman of a different temperament, he would have been an entirely different person. He loved study, it was
true ; but none enjoyed more than he the de-
lights of a family circle. None needed more
than he did the kindness of a wife and children.
She lived with him thirty-four years, and on
the seventeenth day of April, 1834, she sunk
under the disease, consumption, with which
she had been suffering for a long time.

But I am anticipating my story. For two years after his arrival from his last voyage, Mr. Bowditch remained at home, and engaged as a merchant in commerce. We find him generally in connection with his old friend, Capt. Prince, trying his fortunes by adventures of money sent to different parts of the world. He seems to have had no intention of ever again returning to sea. July fourteenth, 1802, he owned one-sixth of a small schooner and its cargo, valued at nine hundred and eleven dollars. During this long residence in town, his fame had increased. He had become known among his fellow-citizens as an " able mathematician." *
He was therefore appointed to offices of honor and trust. He was a member of the school-committee of the town. This boy, who had been obliged to leave school at the age of ten years and three months, was now one to teach others. He was Secretary of the East-India Marine Society of Salem. This society has now one of the most interesting collections of East-Indian curiosities that can be found in America. The association was composed of

* From the Manuscript Journal of a gentleman in Salem.

the most influential men in the town of Salem.
No one could be enrolled among their number
unless he had sailed as captain or supercargo of
a vessel around either Cape Horn or the Cape
of Good Hope. It was intended as a benevo-
lent society, for the relief of the families of de-
ceased members ; and also for the promotion of
the art of navigation. Mr. Bowditch was one
of its active members. In the early part of this
century, the society was accustomed, on its days
of annual meeting, to have a public procession.
A description of one of these processions may
not be uninteresting to you. I quote the words
of an eye-witness of a celebration that occurred
two years later than the period of which I am
speaking, but the date is unimportant, as the
ceremony was the same. " January 4th, 1804.
This day was the annual meeting of the East-
India Marine Society. As the clergy attend in
turn, this occasion afforded me an opportunity
to enjoy the day with them. After business,
but before dinner, they moved in procession ;
but the ice limited the distance. Each of the
brethren bore some Indian curiosity, and the
palanquin was borne by negroes dressed nearly
in the Indian manner. A person dressed in

Chinese habits, and masked, passed in front. The crowd of spectators was great. Several gentlemen were invited to dine. Instrumental music was provided in the town, for the first time, and consisted of a bass-drum, bassoon, clarionet, and flute, and was very acceptable. There was no singing." * * * " It is a most happy arrangement," continues this writer, " to deliver all the papers of this company into the hands of Mr. Nathaniel Bowditch, lately returned from his voyage to India, that they may be prepared for public inspection."

In July, 1802, Mr. Bowditch bought a part of a small vessel engaged in a sealing voyage ; but he lost by this adventure, half of his investment. In September, of the same year, he, with three others, bought the new ship Putnam, built a short time previously, at Danvers ; and, on the twenty-first of November, he sailed as master, and owner of one small part of the whole ship and cargo, valued at fifty-six thousand dollars. Though he went in the capacity of captain, he was determined to do nothing more than direct the course of the ship ; and leave to the officers under him all the labor usually expected of commanders. He made an agreement with two skilful individuals, to take upon themselves these duties. He did so, in order that he might be enabled to pursue his studies more carefully, and without that interruption that must inevitably have occurred, had he been obliged to watch every favorable breeze, or the first appearances of the gathering hurricane. But, as we shall see, whenever real danger called him to duty, he then stood firm, and gave his commands like one who was satisfied that the time required earnestness. A few days after leaving the port of Beverly, he was seen walking " fore and aft " the vessel, with very hurried steps, and deeply absorbed, apparently, in the solution of some problem. The wind had been blowing freshly, for some time ; and, whilst he was meditating, and forgetful of every thing except the problem, the mate of the vessel had been hoping that he would see the severe squall which was coming upon the vessel and was, even then, skimming fiercely over the troubled water. He feared to suggest to him the importance of taking in some of the sails, because the discipline on board ship prevents an inferior officer from interfering with the superior, when the latter is on deck. At length, aroused by the dan-

ger of the vessel, he ventured the remark,
" Captain, would it not be better to take in the
topgallant sails ? " These words aroused Mr.
Bowditch from his reverie, and he instantly ordered all hands to duty ; and fortunately, by his
activity and energy, was enabled to furl the
extra sail before the gust struck the vessel. But
this event taught Mr. B. a lesson ; and he gave
strict orders to the two officers mentioned above,
to waive all ceremony with him, and to take
the command of the ship, whether he was on
deck or not. This rule was always observed,
except on difficult occasions ; and then Mr.
Bowditch assumed the authority of commanding
officer ; and always, by his calmness and sagac-
ity, gained the respect and confidence of those
in employment under him. Before the termination of this voyage, we shall see a strong ex-
ample of this. But now let us proceed on our
expedition with him, and, again cross the Atlantic, pass around the Cape of Good Hope to the
islands of the Indian Ocean. But I should pre-
mise, that, as he had become more acquainted
with various mathematical and philosophical pursuits, he had imported from Europe most of the
great works on these subjects, and he now was

prepared to devote himself more closely than ever to the darling object of his life, the attainment of a knowledge in the truths of science. He was determined, on this voyage, to undertake the investigation and thorough study of one work on the heavens, a book which he had understood was above any thing ever before written by man, on that subject. Imagine, if you can, the zeal and beautiful elevation of feeling with which he must have approached this book upon a subject that had interested him from earliest years. Doubtless, he thought not, then, of the fame he was to gain from it. The name of it you will like to know. I shall speak of it again ; but, meanwhile, I will merely mention that it was called, " A Treatise on the Mechanism of the Heavens,"—(Mecanique Celeste,) and was written in French, by a mathematician named La Place, the greatest scientific man, after Newton, of modern times. But this was not the only work Mr. Bowditch took with him. He had all the most important works which had been published on the same subject, they having been imported for him by a bookseller, named Blunt, in payment of services rendered.

These various studies of course influenced his
Journal. He doubtless was an observer of passing events ; but he recorded less of them than on
the preceding voyages.

By the first record, it appears, that on
" Sunday, November twenty-first, 1802, at one
o'clock, P. M., sailed from Captain Hill's wharf,
in Beverly. At two, passed Baker's Island
lights, with fine and pleasant breeze." This
fair weather lasted but a few days, and by far
the greater part of the voyage was uncomfortable, in consequence of the prevalence of rain
and wind. On January twenty-fifth, 1803, he
saw the islands of Tristan d'Acunha ; and,
whilst coursing along under easy sail, took several observations of them, and made a chart of
their various positions.

On the second of May, he arrived among the
Pepper Islands, near the coast of Sumatra. He
found several American captains there, all actively engaged in loading their vessels with pepper. He had considerable difficulty in making
any arrangement with the Rajahs of different
places ; but at length, having touched without
success at several ports, he began to load at
Tally-poo, on the ninth of May. There he

continued until the eighteenth of July, when, by his Journal, it appears that, having wasted a number of days, expecting that more pepper would be brought to the shore, he was informed by the Rajah he would not be allowed any more. Knowing that he should meet with equal trouble at every place on the coast, he concluded to quit it, and call at the Isle of France, on his homeward passage. During their voyage, amid the various shoals and islands which abound here, they met with no inconvenience and no interruption, save that they anchored once or twice, toward night, and, on the twenty-fifth of July, were obliged to heave to, under the fire of two English ships of war, one named the Royal George, the commander of which took the liberty of searching, for the purpose of seeing whether there were any Englishmen on board. The officer, however, was very polite, and the Putnam soon resumed its course; and, in seventy-two hours more, was on the open sea, under full sail, with the aid of the steady trade-winds of that place and season. On the twenty-fourth of August, the voyager was in sight of the Isle of France. He there met his old friend Bonnefoy, whom he had left

there on his first voyage in 1795, and likewise many American friends. After purchasing
some bags of pepper, and taking on board some
provisions, which employed his time for four days,
he sailed for the last time, from any foreign port,
on Wednesday, August 31st, 1803. The voyage
homeward was very disagreeable, in consequence
of much severe weather. Nothing remarkable
happened to enliven the scene ; but Mr. Bowditch disregarded the storms and waves ; his
mind was calm and tranquil, for he was daily
occupied with his " peaceful mathematics." He
wrote in his Journal but seldom. There is,
however, the following account of the Pepper
Islands. " There are several native ports on
the northwestern coast of Sumatra, where the
Americans trade for pepper, — Analaboo-Sooso,
Tangar, Tally-Poo, Muckie, &c. ; and several
smaller ports, including about fifty miles of the
coast. On your arrival at any of these ports, you
contract with the Datoo for the pepper, and fix
the price. If more than one vessel is at the
port, the pepper which daily comes to the scales
is shared between them, as they can agree ; or
they take it day by day, alternately. Sometimes,
the Datoo contracts to load one vessel before

'any other one takes any, and he holds to his
agreement, as *long as he finds it for his interest, and no longer;* for a handsome present, or
an increase in the price, will prevent any more
pepper from being brought in for several days;
and the person who has made the agreement
must either quit the port, or offer an additional
price.

" The pepper season commences in January,
when they begin to take from the vines the small
kernels at the bottom. In March, April, and
May, is the height of the crop, at which time
the pepper taken from the top of the vines is
larger and more solid than that gathered at an
earlier period; many suppose that the pepper is
all gathered in May; but I was in some of the
gardens in July, and found at the top of the vines
large quantities, which would be ripe in a few
days. The young crop was in considerable for-
wardness at the bottom of the vines. Some
calculate on two crops; but, from the best information I could procure, there is only one.

" The pepper is generally weighed with
American scales and weights, one hundred and
thirty-three and a third pounds to a *peccul.*
What is weighed each day is paid for in the

evening; they (the natives) not being willing to trust their property in the hands of those they deal with. And they ought to be dealt with in the same manner; it not being prudent to pay in advance to the Datoo, as it would be often difficult to get either the pepper or the money again from him. Spanish dollars are the current coin, but they do not take halves or quarters. They have a pang, or piece, of which we could get but eighty for a dollar at Tally-Poo, though at other places they give one hundred or one hundred and twenty for the same."

During the whole voyage, as I have already stated, the weather had been very uncomfortable, The approach to the American coast is at all times hazardous, during the winter. The bold and rough shore, the intense cold and severe snow-storms, which make the day shorter even than common, are so many terrors for the sailor. You may judge of the sadness of the crew of the Putnam, when, after a tedious absence of more than a year, they at length, towards the middle of December, 1803, came near the shoal grounds off Massachusetts, by Nantucket. The sleet and rain had been driving over the ocean wave for many days. No sun appeared to guide them by day ; no star illuminated the night. Groping, as it were, in darkness, they coasted along up the shore, yet not within sight of it, now throwing their sounding line upon Nantucket, and soon afterwards upon George's Shoal. There seemed no end to the storm. At length, on the twenty-fifth of December, they had approached, according to Mr. Bowditch's reckoning, from observation made two days before, near to the outer part of Salem harbor. The night was fast closing in. Mr. Bowditch was observed to be on deck, anxiously looking towards the bow of the vessel, as if in order to see something that would cheer the scene. With clear, decided tones, he gave his orders. The seamen saw, and obeyed in silence. "There is something in the wind," whispered one ; " the *old man* * is above." " Stand every man at his post," is the command ; " and look out for land ahead." The fierce gusts of wind swept over Massachusetts Bay, bearing the vessel irresistibly onwards ; the snow-storm increased, and at every moment the darkness increased. At length, for one moment, the clouds of drifting

* An expression, of which sailors make use, when speaking of the captain of the vessel.

snow-flakes parted, and Mr. Bowditch, with his
mate, who were watching, saw distinctly the
light of Baker's Island. " Light, ho ! on the
larboard bow," was passed from one to the other,
on board that ship, in which were many almost
breathless with suspense. It was but for a moment, and again all was obscured. " I am
right," said Mr. B. ; " the direction in which
we are now steering will lead us soon into Salem
Harbor." His prediction was fulfilled. It was
an extraordinary proof of his skill in navigation.
He had had no opportunity for observing the sun
or moon for two or three days, yet, so accurately
had he marked his position in the ocean, at the last
time of observing, that, by steering in the direction
pointed out by the chart, and observing the rate
at which the vessel moved, he was able to calculate so exactly, that, after seventy-two hours of
darkness, as it were, he came up to the light as
easily as if he had been steering always in open
day, with the object distinctly in view. The
old tars could not restrain their expressions of
admiration ; and as, at nine o'clock in the evening, they dropped anchor in safety from the
gale that was now beating with ten-fold violence
outside of the island, they whispered with one
another, so that he overheard them, "The *old*

man has done well, to-night." It was the
twenty-fifth of December, and, throughout
Christendom, the festival in commemoration of
the birth of the Saviour had been celebrated,
and friends had all been gathered. Sadness
marked their countenances at one home, from
which the husband and friend was absent, and
had been long expected. As the blasts beat
through the streets, and as the family clustered
around the bright shining fire upon the hearth-
stone; as the wind whistled through the case-
ment, the thoughts of the wife were turned from
the fireside to the rough ocean on which her husband was tempest tossed. Many weary weeks
had she watched; but, day after day, had the
sun gone down, and, like Rachel, she could not
be comforted. She feared that he was lost.
One after another of her friends had left her,
late at night, and, finally, she was alone. Suddenly, she springs up from her seat, aroused by
the sound of quick knocking at the street door.
She recognises the tap, and in a few moments
she is hanging on his neck, from whom she was
destined never to be long separated, until death
removed her from him for four years; at the end
of which time, he was placed by death in quiet-
ness at her side.

CHAPTER VII.

THUS finished Mr. Bowditch's career as a sailor, having been, about eight years, engaged in this pursuit. But let us now review a little, and see what he was doing, during these voyages, and how he occupied his time. He was very regular in his habits. During the first two voyages, he attended to the duties of mate of the vessel, and stood his watches. This, of course, prevented him from studying as much as he otherwise would have done. He, moreover, as we have seen, took fewer books with him. But, during the next two voyages, the Captain excused him from the watches, and he was able to read without the smallest interruption. After the deck had been washed in the

morning, he walked for half an hour; he then
went into the cabin to study, until the time
arrived at which he was to observe the sun,
which is done in order to tell whereabouts in
the ocean a vessel is. Having finished this, he
usually dined. After this, he slept a few moments, or took a walk, and then studied again
until tea-time. After supper, he was again at
work until nine, when he used to walk for some
time, cheerfully talking with his comrades. After this, he usually labored until late at night;
and, in order not to disturb his fellow-passengers,
he did not keep a light in the cabin, but frequently stood upon the cabin stairway, reading
by the light of the binnacle lamp, where the
compass was kept. Whenever the vessel arrived at a port, he was still engaged, but in a different way, perhaps. The instant he was freed
from the duties of weighing pepper on the coast
of Sumatra, he went to his books. No time was
wasted, either in foul or fair weather. It made
no difference to him, whether the ship was rest-
ing motionless upon the water, or tossing upon
the heaviest swell, he was always a worker.
But there was yet another and more beautiful
trait still, in his character. He not merely loved

study, himself, but he was determined to persuade all others to love it, also. During his
first voyage, he used to go to the forecastle, or
sailor's cabin, and carry his books of Navigation,
and teach them how to guide a ship by the rules
found in these books. He then went on deck,
and explained to each one the method of using
the quadrant and sextant, two instruments used
by a sea-captain. There is an old man now
living in Salem, who, when speaking of this disposition of Mr. Bowditch, said, " I was the
steward on board the vessel, and Mr. Bowditch
frequently scolded me, because I did not come
to study with him more steadily." It is a fact,
that every sailor on board the ship, during that
voyage, became afterwards captain, and probably
some of them would never have risen so high,
had it not been for the kindness of their friend.
I love to think of this trait in his character. He
delighted in learning, for its own sake, and he
was always pleased when he could find some
one upon whom he could bestow all his acquirements. He had no mean standard of comparison between himself and his fellows, but desired
to give and receive as much good as it was possible for him to bestow or accept.

He was beloved for this by all; but his kindness of heart led him not merely to teach those
who knew less than he, but he was wont to seek
them, when sick, in order to relieve them. One
of them, who lately died, wrote in a letter, after
alluding to his willingness to teach others, " But
the kindness and attention to the poor sea-sick
cabin-boy are to this day (April, 1838,) upper-
most in my memory, and will last, when his
learning is remembered no more." How bright
were his talents and love of study, how beautiful his devotion to others' comfort and improvement ! He might have been as learned, without
displaying this regard for others. But he would
not then have had such tributes of love, as was
displayed by this old sailor, who remembered
his kindness rather than his instruction.

But let us examine his particular studies, pur-
sued while at sea. We have already seen, that,
from a boy, he had loved simple arithmetic, and
on becoming older, had studied deeply in mathematics, a kind of learning similar in character
to arithmetic, only much more difficult and important. During the long voyages to India, he
had ample opportunity for following this branch
of science ; consequently, we find that he was

6

chiefly occupied with that subject. On the
first voyage, he discovered many errors in a
book on Navigation, some of which were so important, that, by their means, not a few vessels
had been shipwrecked. This erroneous work
was originally published in London, by a man
named Hamilton Moore, and it was almost ex-
clusively used by seamen. It had been repub-
lished in America, in 1798, by Mr. Blunt, then
living in Newburyport. One edition was published, and a second was about to be issued, in
1799, when Mr. Blunt learned, by means of a
mutual friend, that Mr. Bowditch, during his
two first voyages, had detected many of these
errors, and was willing to inform him of them.
Mr. Blunt immediately made application to the
young navigator, and received the assistance he
wanted. Finding that Mr. Bowditch had within him the means of rendering essential service,
Mr. Blunt proposed to him, when starting on
his fourth voyage, that is, to India, to examine
all the tables, and see what number of errors he
could find. Mr. Bowditch agreed to the propo-
sal ; and, during this voyage, his time was much
occupied with this task ; a very wearisome, but,
as it proved eventually, a profitable one, as it

regards reputation and pecuniary success. The
mistakes were so numerous, that he found it
much easier to make a new work, and introduce
therein his own improvements ; so that Mr. B.,
before the termination of the voyage, decided
to make some arrangement for this purpose.
The consequence was, that, instead of publishing a third edition of Moore's Navigator, in 1802,
the first edition of the " American Practical
Navigator" was published by Mr. Bowditch,
under his own name, Mr. Blunt being proprie-
tor. Thus was laid, at the age of twenty-nine,
the foundation of a work on navigation, that has
kept constantly before the public, as one of the
best of the kind either in America or England.
It passed through its tenth edition a short time
before Mr. Bowditch's death. Upwards of
thirty thousand copies have been published
since its commencement. It soon superseded
entirely Mr. Moore's, and was early republish-
ed in London. And it was not only obtained
by every American seaman, but even English
ships sought for Bowditch's Navigator, as their
safety during their long voyages. Many amusing anecdotes are related, in reference to this
book. An American captain once took passage

in an English ship, from the Isle of France, for
St. Helena. After being a few days out, the
passenger, about noon, brought on deck his
" Navigator" (one of Bowditch's editions) for
the purpose of using it. While thus engaged,
the English captain of the vessel walked up, and
looked at the work. " Why," says he, " you
use the same work that we do. Pray, where
did you get that? "   And great was the surprise of the Englishman, when he learned that
the author of the book, he was using every day
of his life, was the near neighbor and friend of
the person he was talking with. Little did he
imagine that he was dependent upon the efforts
of a simple son of an American cooper, for the
information by which he was enabled to go from
sea to sea, in comparative safety. But how is
it, that this work has been able to remain so
long one of the best works of the kind? Because
Mr. Bowditch bestowed intense pains upon it,
and with every new edition made all the improvements possible. He moreover brought all
his learning to bear upon it. In the explana-
tions of the rules, he was simple, so that the
most ignorant could understand them. But, in
addition to all this, as we have already stated,

he introduced all the new methods which he himself had discovered. One of these was favorably noticed by a celebrated French astronomer, in a Journal published in 1808.

But, although his attention was much devoted to this book on navigation, he evidently considered it as of little moment, compared with higher objects. During the long voyages, he had been studying the higher branches of knowledge, the difficult calculations of the motions of the heavenly bodies. The deep love he had for these pursuits had a most pleasing effect upon him. If he were sad or disturbed, he sought quiet and cheerfulness in "his peaceful mathematics." As arithmetic had been the darling pursuit of his boyhood, so now the curious and intricate problems of mathematics, or sublime theories of the planets, occupied his best leisure hours. We have seen that, long before going to sea, he studied French, for the purpose of reading a work on mathematics. He continued to read with much interest the works of that country. Some of you may know, that about the close of the last century, at the Revolution in France, all the nation was aroused, every branch of learning and of art received new life. The

consequence was, that a vast many men of the
highest genius arose, and, patronised by government, they put forth to the world extraordinary
works of learning. Most of these, when upon
astronomy, Mr. Bowditch procured for himself,
by means of the publisher of the " Navigator."
He was still engaged in extracting from various
works, or, in other words, in filling up his volumes of manuscripts, though now, from the increase of his property, he was enabled to buy
the originals ; and of course, his manuscripts
were chiefly his sea journals, and the notes
made by himself upon the various authors he
read. But he did not confine himself entirely
to science. He read history, and some works
of a literary character ; although he never spent
much time upon inferior books. " Why read
any thing you cannot speak of ? " he used frequently to say. He likewise studied the Spanish, Italian, and Portuguese languages.

His mode of learning languages is instructive.
As soon as he determined to study one, he
bought a Bible, grammar, and dictionary, in
that tongue. After learning a few of the pro-
nouns and auxiliary verbs, he began to translate,
and usually commenced with the first chapter of

the Gospel of St. John, because in the few first verses there are many repetitions. Having studied them thoroughly, he proceeded to other portions of the Bible, with which he was most acquainted. When at home, he always carried the Bible to church, and used it instead of an English one, during the services. But he had another plan, which is very useful to one who has a bad memory. I will now explain to you one of his vocabularies, or collections of words with their meanings attached thereto, so arranged, that he could refer much more easily to them than to a common dictionary. Although he did not learn German until a long time after the period of his life which we are now speaking of, still, as the German vocabulary is the most perfect, I will describe it. It is made upon two large sheets, one foot broad and more than a foot and a half high, which, with the inside of the covers, make six pages. The pages are divided into columns, about one and a half inches wide ; that is, large enough to admit, in very small writing, a word with its signification by its side. Of course, the columns are divided for the letters of the alphabet in a manner proportioned to the number of pages of each letter in the dictionary. Having thus prepared his book, whenever he found that he was obliged (for want of memory) to look at the dictionary more than once for the signification of a word, he wrote it in his vocabulary ; and, by the act of writing, strengthened, in some measure, his memory of that word, and moreover, he could turn to it immediately, and not lose time in turning over the leaves of a larger book. The number of words thus seen at a glance, as it were, is remarkable. In the above-described six pages, there are eleven thousand German words, all written distinctly, but in small letters, and without any repetitions, and with as many abbreviations as he himself chose. I have been thus minute upon this subject, not because I think that all ought to make vocabularies, but because some may be benefited, some, for instance, who have bad memories. Moreover, I wished to speak to you of them, as marks of his perseverance.

Two important events took place during this period of Mr. Bowditch's life, which it becomes our duty to record. On the twenty-eighth day of May, 1799, he was chosen a member of the American Academy of Arts and Sciences.

This Society was the first which bestowed upon him the honor of membership of its body. It is composed of men of science, combined for the purpose of improving themselves and the community in knowledge. He continued a member of this body during his life; and, subsequently, in May, 1829, just thirty years after becoming a member, he was chosen its President, in which office he was continued until the day of his death.

Another honor, and one which was more pleasant to him than any received at any time afterwards, was bestowed during this period. In 1802, his ship was wind-bound in Boston, and he left it, for the purpose of attending the annual commencement at Cambridge College. He knew but few individuals there, though he had corresponded with some of the Professors; and one of the Corporation of the College, Chief Justice Parsons, was one of his kindest friends. He went alone, and, while listening in the crowd to the names of those upon whom the honors were conferred, he thought he heard his own pronounced, but he supposed that he might have been mistaken, inasmuch as the notice was given in Latin. But how great was his emotion,

when he heard from a friend that his suspicions
were well founded! It was to him the proudest
day of his life. And we, who know his humble
origin, his simplicity and modesty, can in some
measure understand the thrill of pleasure that
must have run through him, when he found himself thus noticed by the first and oldest University in the land. And why was he thus noticed?
Because he had well improved the hours of his
life; because his days and nights had been spent
in activity and earnest study. In after-life,
when his fame was established, and the great
societies of Europe all bestowed upon him their
diplomas, he always looked upon them as of
small moment, compared with this his first,
earliest proof of esteem from his fellow-men.

Having now completed his sea-life, let us
enter upon his new scene of energy and benevolence, as a citizen and father; and our next
chapter will include several years of his life in
Salem.

CHAPTER VIII.

MR. BOWDITCH, on his arrival from sea,
met with one of those events to which he always
referred, when any one doubted the expediency
of any kind of knowledge. In his voyages to
Portugal and Spain, he had become acquainted
with the Spanish language. It so happened,
that no one else in Salem was acquainted with
it ; and an important paper came to the care of
a sturdy and sensible old sea-captain, but it was
unfortunately unintelligible to him, for it was
written in this same unknown tongue. A friend
suggested to him that probably Mr. Bowditch

would decipher it for him.   The document was
handed to Mr. Bowditch, who in a few days
returned it with a free English translation accompanying it.   The old sailor was delighted,
and immediately supposed that any one who
knew so much about a foreign language must be
a very superior person, and capable of perform-
ing any duties.   Moreover, he was delighted
with the apparent generosity of Mr. Bowditch,
in making the translation without charge to his
employer.   It happened at this time, that an
Insurance Office in Salem was in need of a
President.   The Captain was one of the directors of this Institution, and immediately used all
his influence in promoting the election of his
young friend.   This influence succeeded, and,
in 1804, we find Mr. Bowditch installed as
President of the Essex Fire and Marine Insurance Company.   In this office he continued,
with entire success, until 1823, when he removed to Boston, and took charge of other
similar but much larger institutions.   The relief
was great, which he experienced from not being
obliged to seek subsistence for his family by en-
gaging in the sailor's life.   The duties of the
office in which he now engaged *seemed* to oc-

cupy all his time, yet he still did not neglect science. He arose at six in the morning, during the year; and took a walk, either before or after breakfast, of at least two miles. At nine o'clock he went to the office, and there he continued until one. After another walk, he dined, and, after a short sleep, he again visited his office until tea-time. From tea-time until nine in the evening, he was at his duties, and amid business. Now, it is very certain that he was not all the time, during office hours, actually engaged in business, but he was constantly liable to interruption, as much as he had been when an apprentice. Yet he found leisure enough for study, by early rising and regular habits. He used to say, "Before nine o'clock in the morning, 1 learned all my mathematics." He kept some of his books on philosophy at his office, and, whenever a moment of leisure recurred, he was busily occupied in science. At home, he had no private room for many years; and, as his family of young children grew up around him, he studied at his simple pine desk, in the midst of their noise and play. He was never disturbed, except when they failed in kindness to one another, and then he could never con-

tinue to study until quiet was restored. In
truth, the influence of his studies was felt by
his children, whose greatest reward was to receive from him, in token of his approbation, the
drawings of various constellations upon their
arms or forehead. It was a sad day for them,
when they did not receive from his pen the rep-
resentation of the Belt of Orion, or of some
other beautiful appearance in the heavens.

But, in addition to the duties of his office, he
had began to be interested in the political affairs
of the day. After the Revolution, and the new
government of the country went into operation
under the Presidency of General Washington,
there had been but little political excitement in
Essex county. There were no great parties,
which were destined soon afterwards to spring
up, and excite the bitterest animosity between
individuals who had been from birth the warm-
est friends. It would be impossible, were it useful, to tell all the causes that led to the formation
of the two great sects in politics, called the Federalists and Republicans. Suffice it to say, that
even during Washington's connexion with the
government, the seeds of this division were beginning to spring up; and, upon the accession

of Mr. Adams, the father of John Quincy
Adams who is now living, the rancor increased
with tenfold energy, until at length the Republican party triumphed in the election of Thomas
Jefferson to the office of President of the United
States. In Salem, the violence of party spirit
rose as high as in any city of the Union. It
would have been surprising, with his desire for
aiding any public cause, if Mr. Bowditch had
not been influenced by the excitements of the
day. He was much interested in them ; and,
in the note-books upon science, we find frequently brief memoranda of the results of an
election at the bottom of a page, or at the end
of some theorem. He was moreover, for two
years, a member of the State Council. He was
likewise proposed by the Federalists as a repre-
sentative to the General Court, but at that election they were defeated.

We have scarcely any idea of the rancor
with which the two parties contended. Persons
who had been, during life, sincere and devoted
friends, were separated by this virulence. Mr.
Bowditch suffered as much as others, on this
account, and two of his longest and best-tried
friends he did not have any intercourse with, for

many years. Dr. Bentley and Captain Prince were these persons, and with both of them you are already acquainted. It was not until 1817, when President Monroe visited these northern States, that harmony was restored between the two great divisions, and friends once more embraced each other. But, in the midst of all this excitement with politics, Mr. Bowditch never neglected the duties of his office, or the study of science. In fact, the pursuit of learning had, as before, a sweet influence over his character. It still made him calm and serene. An illustration of this you may find in what follows. In 1812, after a long series of supposed insults and wrongs from Great Britain, the American government declared war against that power. Mr. Bowditch was completely overcome by the news, and for two days was so much distressed, that he was unable to study. Friends who knew him had never seen him look so saddened before, on any public emergency. He could speak of nothing but the disasters that he foresaw war would entail upon his country. On the morning of the third day, he arose, and, descending into the parlor, said to his wife, "It won't do for me to continue thus. I *will not* think any

more about it." Saying this, he retired again
to his books. The difference in his whole manner was very perceptible. He rarely afterward
allowed himself to be disturbed by the unfortunate state of affairs; and, amid the placid
thoughts excited in him by science, he found
certain rest. Such should be the benign influence of study upon every one.

Amid all these various engagements, he was
full of sympathy for others. Wherever he saw
he could aid with his counsel, he did so; and
many widows and orphans have felt the influence of his charity. This charity showed itself
chiefly in a desire to improve others. There
was scarcely one of those connected with him,
in friendship, upon whom he did not devote some
time for their instruction. To one young lady
he taught French, and another studied Italian
with him. If a young man needed funds, he
knew upon whom he could call with a certainty
of substantial aid; for throughout life, it was one
of the remarkable attributes of Mr. Bowditch's
character, that he could persuade many to open
their hearts to the poor, who, upon other occasions, were deaf to the common feelings of humanity. For one young person of this kind,

Mr. B. obtained a subscription sufficient to enable him to continue at the university, whereas his young friend would have been unable to do so, without assistance. He was always so zealous in these undertakings, that no one felt under any obligations to him. It was his delight to help, and every one saw that his heart was engaged in the cause. His zeal for humanity was at times immoderate, and the following laughable law case occurred in consequence cf it. One day, he was informed that a little girl who lived with him had been run over by some careless driver, and a crowd, which he could perceive at a little distance from him, was a collection of individuals drawn together on her account. He immediately ran forward, and getting to the outside of the circle, began very energetically to make his way into it. In doing so, he pulled one of the bystanders so forcibly, that the individual, as it will appear in the sequel, was offended. Arriving, however, by dint of hard pushing, at the object of his search, he took his little domestic with him, and guided her safely home. On the next day, he was much surprised at receiving a summons from a justice of the peace, to appear before him, to answer to

the charge of assault and battery upon the individual above-mentioned. He answered the call,
and paid his fine of a few dollars; but the judge,
who had been notorious for always making both
parties suffer, when it was possible for himself to
gain thereby, said, on receiving the fine, " But
you say that Mr. —— *pushed* you, after you
had *pulled* him." " I did sir." " Very well,
then if you wish to complain of him, I will fine
him, likewise." The ludicrous nature of the
whole action struck Mr. Bowditch so forcibly,
that he was not unwilling to increase the folly of
it. The plaintiff was then fined, and the affair
was ended. It is but right to say, that the judge
was considered, previous to this, one entirely
unfit for the office. Probably no other would
have issued a summons on such an occasion;
and the plaintiff was not unjustly punished for
having called upon such a person to aid him in
prosecuting an individual who, in exerting himself to help another, had slightly disarranged the
dress of a bystander.

Mr. Bowditch's desire to aid the unfortunate
was exhibited on another occasion, when a poor,
overladen horse was the object of his commisera-
tion. A truckman had been violently beating

the animal, in order to induce him to pull along
a very heavy load, which was too large for his
strength.   Mr. B. had watched the driver for
some time, and at length he ran vehemently forward, and in abrupt and decided tones ordered
him to desist.   The truckman was much superior to Mr. Bowditch in personal strength, and
was, at first, disposed to ridicule the attempt of
his inferior to restrain him.   Full of indigna-
tion, Mr. B. exclaimed, " If you dare touch
that horse again, and if you do not immediately
go and get another to assist him, I will appeal
to the law, and you will see which of us two
will conquer."   The man yielded, and Mr. B.
passed away.

The public institutions of the town all felt his
influence.   The East-India Marine Society, of
which I have already spoken, improved very
much under his auspices, as President.   It had
fallen considerably during high political times,
and, when he was chosen chief officer, he in-
stilled such zeal among the younger members
of it, and obtained so many new members that
it revived, and, soon after his removal to Boston, the splendid hall was erected, containing

the most remarkable collection of East-India curiosities, of which I spoke in chapter sixth.

The libraries he had always felt very much interested in. You already know what reason he had for being devoted to the Philosophical Library, for from it he drew most of his knowledge of science. But there was another, which had been in existence much longer than this, called the Social Library. The books contained in these two collections were almost wholly distinct in their characters. In one, only works of science were to be found; while the other was chiefly devoted to literature. Mr. Bowditch saw that both of them united would be of great service to the community; for it would not merely combine the books, but the energies of the proprietors. Consequently, it appears that he, with another of the Philosophical Library proprietors, was chosen a committee for the purpose of providing for a union. This was happily effected, 1810; and the Salem Athenæum arose from the combination. The rooms over his office were chosen as the place for their deposit; and for many years, he was one of the most active of the Trustees.

There was another institution, with which he was intimately connected during the whole of the time he lived in Salem ; I allude to the church in which his early friend, Rev. Dr. Prince, officiated. He was one of the committee of the parish ; and, though never a member of the church, strictly so called, he was a constant attendant upon the services, and had great influence in keeping up the harmony and supporting the true dignity of the congregation.

In the performance of his duties as President of the Insurance Company, he was ever faithful and true. His desire was, to know the truth and to act up to it. He was frequently placed in circumstances which required great decision. At times, a disposition was shown to deceive him ; at others, a similar one was shown by a richer stockholder to gain advantages over a poorer one. I well remember an anecdote in which it is said a purse-proud rich man strove to browbeat him into doing an act which Mr. B. thought would be unjust to another poorer one. The nabob pleaded his riches, and amount of stock, and intimated that he would have his way. " No, sir, you won't. I stand here in this place to see justice done, and, as long as I

am here, I will defend the weak." He seldom
met with difficulties of this kind, for few dared
approach him with the intention to be unjust or
untrue. Nothing aroused him so much to an
almost lion fierceness, as any appearance of
wickedness in the transaction of public business.
He had much wisdom likewise in the selection
of risks, so that the office, while under his control, succeeded admirably, and he left it pros-
perous.

During his residence in Salem, he was frequently invited to seats of honor and trust. We
have already mentioned his political course. In
1806, by the agency of Chief Justice Parsons,
then in the Corporation of Harvard College, he
was appointed Professor of Mathematics in that
University. In 1818, he was requested by
President Jefferson, in very flattering terms, to
accept of a similar office in the University of
Virginia. In 1820, he was called upon by the
Secretary of War of the United States, to consent to an appointment at the Public Military
School at West Point. All of these he refused,
as not congenial to his mind. He always de-
clined talking in public. He would teach all
who came to him, but he could not deliver a

public course of lectures. His extreme modesty prevented. For it will be remembered, that he was as remarkable, from his youth, for his modesty, amounting, in early life, to diffidence, as he was for his other qualities. Moreover, it should be stated that, at times, he had a certain hesitation in his mode of speaking, which probably would have prevented him from addressing easily a public audience.

In 1818, he was urged to take charge of an Insurance Office in Boston, but he preferred living in his native place.

CHAPTER IX.

[*From* 1803 *to* 1823, — *aged* 30 — 50.]

Papers published by Mr. B. in the Memoirs of the Academy : account of some of them. — Total eclipse of the sun in 1806 : effect of it. — Anecdote of Chief Justice Parsons. — Meteor that fell over Weston, Ct. : account of its curious appearance : effect of these papers upon his fame in Europe. — Chosen member of most of the learned societies of the Old World. — Quits Salem, to become connected with larger institutions in Boston.

It should be remembered, that, during these stormy political times, Mr. Bowditch was chiefly engaged in making his notes on the great work to which we have already alluded, La Place's " Mecanique Celeste ; " and that it was between the years 1800 and 1820, that is, during this same time, that he wrote twenty-three papers, which were published in the Memoirs of the American Academy of Arts and Sciences. Of some of these last, I will give you an account. Of the others, were I to mention them, you could understand but little. They relate chiefly to observations made upon the moon ; the comets of 1807 and 1811 ; the eclipses of the sun, which took place in 1806 and 1811 ; meas-

urements of the height of the White Mountains
in New Hampshire; observations on the compass ; on a pendulum supported by two points ;
and the correction of some mistakes in one of
the books studied first by him in early life,
called Newton's " Principia." A few of these
papers I will, in some measure, explain to you.
I commence with his observation upon a total
eclipse of the sun, which occurred June 16,
1806. I shall quote nearly the words of the
observer. " On the day of the eclipse, the
weather was remarkably fine, scarcely a cloud
being visible in any part of the heavens. I
made preparations for the observations in the
garden adjoining the house in which I reside,
near the northern part of Summer street, in
Salem. Having been disappointed in procuring
a telescope of a large magnifying power, I was
obliged to make use of that attached to my the-
odolite, which gave very distinct vision, though its
magnifying power was small. An assistant was
seated near me, who counted the seconds from
a chronometer, and thus enabled me to mark
down with a pencil the time when the first impression was made on the sun, without taking
my eye from the telescope, till four or five sec-

onds had elapsed, and the eclipse had sensibly increased ; after which I examined the second and minute hands of the chronometer, and took every precaution to prevent mistakes. Four or five minutes before the commencement of the eclipse, I began to observe that part of the sun where the first contact [of the moon's shadow] was expected to take place ; and eight minutes twenty-eight seconds after ten o'clock, I observed the first impression. As the eclipse advanced, there did not appear to be so great a diminution of the light as was generally expected ; and it was not till the sun was nearly covered, that the darkness was very sensible. The last ray of light disappeared instantaneously. The moon was then seen surrounded by a luminous appearance of considerable extent, such as has been generally taken notice of in total eclipses of the sun." A number of stars became visible. The observer mentions that the light in the garden was not entirely gone ; but in the house, candles were needed, as if it were evening. At thirty-two minutes eighteen seconds after eleven o'clock, that is, at a little more than an hour from the beginning of the eclipse, the first returning ray of light burst forth, with great splendor. I have heard the effect, described by those who saw it, as surpassingly grand. Suddenly, the light of midday seemed to break in upon the quiet of evening. So completely were all the animal creation deceived, that the cows returned lowing homeward, and the fowls sought their roosts, and quietly placed their heads under their wings. All human beings were looking in mute amazement, and deep silence prevailed, as the dark shadow of the moon came stealing over the surface of the sun, at noon. There was something fearful about the total obscuration of the luminary. Suddenly, this beautiful ray of burning light shot forth, 'mid heaven, and fell upon the earth, and with it arose a loud shout from the assembled crowd, and aged men * and women joined in the chorus, and saluted again the orb of day.

This paper, though short, is one of the most important he ever wrote. In a note to it, he first mentions publicly a mistake he had discovered in the " Mecanique Celeste."

---

* Chief Justice Parsons, it is said, used to mention that moment as one of the most exciting of his life ; and he could not forbear throwing up his hat, and joining in the shout with which the boys saluted the first returning light of the sun.

In 1815, Mr. Bowditch published another paper, which I may be able to explain to you in some degree. You have all heard of falling stars, or meteors, and probably most of you have seen them frequently, when walking at night, when the sky is clear. Some of these are very small ; they seem at a great distance. They suddenly appear in our heavens, and as suddenly disappear, and nothing more is heard or seen of them. Others, on the contrary, appear larger, and fall to the earth, after having traversed a great portion of the heavens. On the fourteenth of December, 1807, one of the most curious exploded, and fell over Weston, in Connecticut. Mr. B., in his Memoir, writes thus :

" The extraordinary meteor which appeared at Weston, in Connecticut, on the fourteenth of December, 1807, and exploded with several discharges of stones, having excited great attention throughout the United States, and being one of those phenomena of which few exact observations are to be found in the history of physical science, I have thought that a collection of the best observations of its appearance at different places, with the necessary deductions for determining, as accurately as possible, the

height, direction, velocity, and magnitude, of
the body, would not be unacceptable to the
Academy, since facts of this kind, besides being
objects of great curiosity, may be useful in the
investigation of the origin and nature of these
meteors; and as the methods of making these
calculations are not fully explained in any treatise of trigonometry common in this country, I
have given the solutions of two of the most necessary problems, with examples calculated at
full length. The second problem is not (to my
knowledge) given in any treatise of spherics.
The observations of the meteor which, after
many inquiries, were found to have been made
with sufficient accuracy to be introduced in the
present investigation, were those made at Wenham, about seven miles northeasterly of Salem, by Mrs. Gardner, a very intelligent lady,
who had an opportunity of observing it with
great attention; those at Weston, by Judge
Wheeler and Mr. Staples; and those at Rutland, in Vermont, by William Page, Esq."
After giving the requisite solutions, he pro-
ceeds: " Some time after the appearance of
the meteor, I went with Mr. Pickering to Mrs.
Gardner's house, at Wenham, where she had

observed the phenomenon. She informed us, that on the morning of the fourteenth of December, 1807, when she arose, she went towards the window of her chamber, which looks to the westward, for the purpose of observing the weather, according to her invariable practice, for many years past. The sky was clear, except a few thin clouds in the west. It was past daybreak, and, by estimation, about half an hour before sunrise, or seven o'clock. The meteor was immediately observed, just over the southern part of the barn in her farm-yard, nearly in front of the window ; its disc was well defined ; and it resembled the moon so much, that, unprepared as Mrs. G.'s mind was for a phenomenon of that nature, she was not at first aware that it was not the moon, till she perceived it in motion, when her first thought (to use her own words) was, ' Where is the moon going to ? ' The reflection, however, was hardly made, when she corrected herself ; and with her eye followed the body with the closest attention throughout its whole course. It moved in a direction nearly parallel to the horizon, and disappeared behind a cloud northward of the house of Samuel Blanchard, Esq. She supposed the meteor to have been visible about half a minute.

" The attention of Judge Wheeler was first drawn by a sudden flash of light, which illuminated every object. Looking up, he discovered in the north a globe of fire just then passing behind the cloud which obscured, though it did not entirely hide, the meteor. In this situation, its appearance was distinct and well defined, like that of the sun seen through a mist. It rose from the north, and proceeded in a direction nearly perpendicular to the horizon, but inclining, by a very small angle, to the west, and deviating a little from the plane of a great circle, but in pretty large curves, sometimes on one side of the plane, and sometimes on the other, but never making an angle with it of more than four or five degrees. Its apparent diameter was about one half or two thirds the apparent diameter of the full moon. It progress was not so rapid as that of common meteors and shooting stars. When it passed behind the thinner clouds, it appeared brighter than before ; and when it passed the spots of clear sky, it flashed with a vivid light, yet not so intense as the light-ning of a thunderstorm. Where it was not too much obscured by thick clouds, a waving, conical train of paler light was seen to attend it, in length about ten or twelve diameters of the body. In the clear sky, a brisk scintillation was observed about the body of the meteor, like that of a burning firebrand carried against the wind. It disappeared about fifteen degrees short of the zenith, and about the same number of degrees west of the meridian. It did not vanish instantaneously, but grew, pretty rapidly, fainter and fainter, as a red-hot cannon-ball would do, if cooling in the dark, only with much more rapidity. The whole period between its first appearance and total extinction was estimated at about thirty seconds. About thirty or forty seconds after this, three loud and distinct reports, like those of a four-pounder near at hand, were heard. Then followed a rapid succession of reports less loud, so as to produce a continued rumbling. This noise continued about as long as the body was in rising, and died away, apparently, in the direction from which the meteor came. Mr. Staples observed, that when the meteor disappeared, there were apparently three succes-

8

sive efforts or leaps of the fire-ball, which grew
more dim at every throe, and disappeared with
the last. From the various accounts which we
have received of the appearance of the body, at
different places, we are inclined to believe that
the time between the disappearance and report,
as estimated by Judge Wheeler, is too little, and
that a minute is the least time that could have
intervened.

"The observations made at Rutland were
procured by the kind offices of Professor Hall,
of Middlebury College, Vermont, to whom Mr.
Page communicated his valuable observations
in a paper expressed in the following terms. ' I
was at the west door of my house on Monday
morning, the fourteenth of December, 1807,
about daylight, and perceiving the sky suddenly
illuminated, I raised my eyes, and beheld a meteor of a circular form in the southwesterly part
of the heavens, rapidly descending to the south,
leaving behind it a vivid, sparkling train of light.
The atmosphere near the south part of the horizon was very hazy; but the passage of the
meteor behind the clouds was visible until it
descended below the mountains, about twenty
miles south of this place. There were white

fleecy clouds scattered about the sky ; but none
so dense as to obscure the track of the meteor.
I now lament that I did not make more particular observations at the time, and I should probably, until this day, have considered it to be what
is commonly called a 'falling star,' had I not
read in the New York papers an account of the
explosion of a meteor, and the falling of some
meteoric stones, near New Haven, Connecticut,
which, by recurring to circumstances then fresh
in my recollection, I found to be on the same
morning that I observed the meteor at Rutland.
I am indebted to my learned friend, Dr. Samuel
Williams, for his aid and directions in ascertain-
ing the situation of the meteor, when I first observed it, and its course, and also for the order
of my observations : — Form, circular ; magnitude, less than a quarter of the diameter of the
moon ; color, red, vivid light ; tail, or train of
light, about eight times the length of its diameter,
at the least, projected opposite to its course.' "

I quote these, to give you some notion of the
appearance of this meteor, and likewise of Mr.
B.'s diligence. From the examination of all
the accounts given him, he came to the conclusion, that the body moved at the rate of more

than three miles per second, and at the height
of eighteen miles above the surface of the earth.
With regard to the magnitude of the body, the
results were less accurate ; and the probability
is, that all the body did not fall, but merely
passed through the air, and continued on its
course into unknown regions of space.

The other papers I shall not mention, because
they are upon subjects difficult to be compre-
hended. The last appeared in the volumes of
the Memoirs of the Academy, published in
1820. All these papers were read by the astronomers and mathematicians of Europe, and
the consequence was, that he was chosen a member of many of the learned societies instituted
there for the promotion of science. In 1818,
he was chosen member of the Royal Societies
of London and Edinburgh ; and, in the year following, was enrolled on the list of the Royal
Irish Academy. While I am upon this subject, I would state, that he afterwards was
elected associate of the Astronomical Society of
London, of the Academies of Berlin and Paler-
mo, and had a correspondence with most of the
astronomers of Europe. The National Insti-
tute of France was about choosing him one of

its foreign members, only eight of which are
chosen from the whole world, when he died.

In addition to the papers to the Academy,
Mr. Bowditch published several articles in re-
views, &c.   One of them is an interesting history of modern astronomy, which is intended to
give us an account of the lives and doings of
the most celebrated astronomers of modern
times.   Such were the principal literary labors
of Mr. Bowditch, during his residence in Salem.

But he was destined soon to leave Salem.
In 1823, overtures were made to him to control
two institutions in Boston, one for Life Insurance, the other for Marine risks.   The offers
were too liberal for him to refuse.   His duties to
his family led him to consent to do what nothing
else could.   On his determination being known,
his fellow-citizens collected together, and paid
him a pleasant tribute of respect and love, by
inviting him to a public and farewell dinner.

As the family left Salem, Mr. Bowditch and
his wife often thought that, after remaining eight
or ten years at Boston, they would return, in
order that their bodies might be laid by the side
of those of their ancestors.   But new friends
awaited them in Boston ; new ties were formed

there ; and, although they always looked to their
native place as the seat of many of their most
beloved associations, they both lived in Boston
until their deaths.

His engagements of a public nature, during
his residence in Boston, were similar to those he
had whilst at Salem.   For many years he man-
aged both institutions.   But, the directors, finding that the duties of one were sufficient to
occupy all his attention, broke up the Marine
Insurance Company, and Mr. Bowditch (or Dr.
Bowditch, as he was now generally called, having received the degree of Doctor of Laws from
Harvard University in 1816) devoted himself to
the Life Insurance Office.   This he raised to
be one of the greatest institutions in New England.   By an alteration in the charter proposed
by Dr. Bowditch, this is now a great Savings
Bank, where immense sums are yearly put in
trust, for widows and orphans.   The only difference in his habits caused by his removal to Boston, was an enlargement of his sphere of labor.
All objects of public utility still engaged his
attention.

The system of popular lectures, of which
we have now so many, commenced with the

Mechanic Institution, of which he was the first President. He was zealous for the improvement of the Boston Athenæum, and was the means of getting for it large sums of money, and of making it more liberal to the public.

An honor was conferred upon him, after his arrival in Boston, which he thought the greatest he ever had attained. Having received two honorary degrees from Harvard University, and having been one of the Board of Overseers of that Institution for many years, he was finally chosen a member of the Corporation, or council of seven men, who guide the whole of the concerns of that important institution. How different the commencement and termination of the career of the poor son of a cooper, who, at ten years of age, left school, and yet, at the end of life was one of the chief directors in the first literary institution in America! And his schoolmates, who laughed at him for his poverty, and thin, coarse dress, where were they?

CHAPTER X.

Sketch of the Life of La Place, author of the " Mecanique
    Celeste." — Newton's labors. — Halley's comet. — The
    importance of astronomy to navigation. — Comets: Dr.
    Bowditch's labors upon this work : difficulties attending
    the undertaking : objects he had in view: first volume
    analysed : Newton's error pointed out.

IN a former part of this story of his life, you
will remember that I stated that, on his last
voyage, Dr. Bowditch commenced his notes
upon the " Mecanique Celeste" of La Place.
It was on the first day of November, during his
disagreeable voyage homewards, in 1803, that
he wrote his first note to the work which was
destined to occupy much of his time from that
moment until his death, thirty-five years afterwards, in Boston. This work certainly deserves
some of our attention, if he thought it worthy of
receiving the attention of so many years of his
life. A brief account of the life of the author
of the original work may interest you, and will
serve as an introduction to the book itself.

Pierre Lucien La Place was born on the
twenty-third of March, 1749, at Beaumont, on
the borders of the beautiful and fertile country

of ancient Normandy, situated in the northwestern part of France.   He was the son of simple
peasants in that country, and, from his earliest
years, was remarkable for the extraordinary powers of memory and intense love of study with
which he was endowed.   In early life every
branch of learning was delightful to him.   He
seemed eager to gain knowledge merely, without regard to the object of his study.   But he
soon began to distinguish himself upon the subject of theology.   This pursuit, however, was
soon ended, and, by some means, of which no
details now remain, his mind was led to mathematics ; and, from that moment, he was devoted
to them.   After spending his youth at his native
place, and having taught mathematics there, he,
at the age of eighteen years, went to Paris, to
seek a wider sphere of knowledge.   Bearing
several letters of recommendation, as a youth of
great promise, he presented himself at the abode
of D'Alembert, who at that time was the first
mathematician of France, and contended with
Euler, at Berlin, for the honor of being the first
in the world.   But the letters upon which the
youth depended so much, proved of no avail.
D'Alembert passed them by in silent neglect,

without even deigning to receive at his own abode the bearer of them. But La Place was fully bent upon success, and, relying upon the force of his own genius as a more powerful recommendation than any letters, he sent to D' Alembert an essay, written by himself, upon a very abstruse subject, relating to mechanics. The Professor, struck with its elegance and deep learning, immediately called upon the writer, and addressed him in these words : " You see, sir, that I think recommendations are worth but very little, and for yourself they are wholly unnecessary. By your own writings you can make yourself better known than by any other means. They are sufficient. I will do all I can for you." In a few days after this conversation, the young man was appointed professor of mathematics in the public military school, at the capital of France. From this period, until the end of his life, he was occupied upon the science which he was called at this early age to teach publicly at Paris. He became daily more acquainted with the great men of the nation, and was himself making additions to the scientific acquirements of the age, thus giving eminent proofs of his activity of mind. He

was a member of the French Academy, or society of learned men, united for the purpose of
advancing the cause of learning, and he stood
soon very high amongst them.

His chief work, the " Celestial Mechanics,"
" Mecanique Celeste,") he began to publish in
1799, and finished the fourth volume in 1805.
This placed him much above all his contempora-
ies ; for in it he had not only combined many
things which he himself had discovered, but likewise gave a history, as it were, of all that had
been done by geometricians from the time of
Sir Isaac Newton until his own day. La Place
found many things, detached, but his genius
proved that many apparently discordant facts
could be explained by Newton's theory of uni-
versal gravitation. His labor must have been
immense. All Europe rung with the fame of
his production, which was said to be beyond
any thing ever performed before by man. The
echo of its fame reached America, and Mr.
Bowditch sought for the volumes, as they were
successively published. The first two he received in part payment of his labor on the
' Navigator."

Soon after his arrival home from his fourth voyage, Dr. Bowditch was taking his accustomed walk towards the lower part of the town of Salem and met his old friend, Captain Prince. They entered into conversation, and Dr. B. remarked that he had, a short time before, received a book from France, which he had longed to obtain, having heard that it was superior to any thing ever before written by man, and which very few were able to comprehend. This work was that which now renders his own name familiarly known among the great men of the earth.

Later in life, La Place published a work, called the "System of the World." In this, which comparatively speaking, is not difficult to be read by almost any one, he attempts to give a plain and simple statement of all that is known in regard to those wise and magnificent laws whereby this solar system is kept together in perfect harmony, while at the same time it is sailing onward through fields of space.

La Place, however, was not a truly great man, because he was not just; he was willing to attribute to himself the discoveries of others. Moreover, there was none of the sweetness of humility about him. On Napoleon Bonaparte's

becoming First Consul in France, La Place
was made one of the ministers of the state ; but
he was found to be unfit for the office, and retired after a few weeks' service, but was made
a member of the Senate, of which he became
President. After finishing his political career,
he published other works of great moment, but
of those I shall not speak. About the year
1827, he was seized with an acute disorder,
which soon terminated his life. His last words
are remarkable, as conveying the same truth
that every wise man has upon his lips at the
hour of death. As he reviewed the amount
of his learning, which was in one respect greater
than that of any man living, he exclaimed,
" What we know here is very little, but what
we are ignorant of is immense." Every man is
compelled to become silent and modest, as he
sees death approach. La Place was like other
common men. He died as a man, and was
buried, and the men of science felt sad, that one
so learned, and of so strong an intellect, should
have departed ; yet, alas, that we should say,
few loved him. I have already stated that the
reason of it was, his low ambition. Endowed
by the Almighty with the loftiest powers of in-

tellect, he stood alone, and commanded the respect of his associates ; but, instead of using his intellect always nobly, he suffered his soul to be degraded by a love of paltry show, and with the gratification of a merely selfish vanity, to gain which, he was at times guilty of injustice to others.   Dr. Bowditch, though he regarded La Place as the greatest mathematician that had ever lived, had little real sympathy with his character.

We must now undertake to give you a short account of the " Mecanique Celeste," and of Dr. Bowditch's labors upon it.   The origina work consists of five volumes, but Dr. Bowditch lived to complete the translation of, and com mentary upon, only the first four.   There are about fifteen hundred pages in the original while there are three thousand eight hundred and eighteen in the American translation.   The object of the original work may be known from the following introductory remarks by the author, on the occasion of printing the first volume, in 1798 : " Newton, towards the end of the last century, published his discovery of the laws of gravity, or of the power by which the solar system is held together.   Since that period, geometricians have succeeded in bringing under this law all the known phenomena of the system of the universe. I mean to bring together those scattered themes and facts upon this subject, so as to form one whole, which shall embrace all the known results of gravity upon the motions, forms, &c., of the fluid and solid bodies that compose our solar system, as well as of those other similar systems that are spread around in the immensity of space." You probably all understand from this quotation the general object of the "Mecanique Celeste." La Place likewise informs us, that the work is divided into two parts. In the first, he proposes to give the methods for determining the motions of the heavenly bodies, their forms, the motions of the oceans and seas upon their surfaces, and finally, the movements of rotation of these spheres about their own axis. In the second part, he promises to apply the rules which he has discovered in the first, to the planets and the satellites which move around them, and likewise to the comets. The first part is found in the first two volumes, the second part occupies the two last. From these few remarks, you will perceive the immense task imposed upon himself by La

Place, and at the same time the grandeur of it.
How wonderful, that a simple man dares attempt to mark out the course of the bright lumi-
naries of heaven, which we see clustering around
us at night! But how much more wonderful
does man become, when we perceive that he has
the *power* to foretell to us the return of comets,
that have never been seen by any one living
now; comets, that have been, during our lives,
travelling into the far-off fields of space ! Strange,
that a simple man can prophesy, to a day, their
return ! Many of you doubtless remember a
beautifully bright and clear comet, which a few
years ago appeared, as had been predicted, after
an absence of seventy-six years. It is called
Halley's comet, after its first discoverer. At
first, it seemed like a bright speck in the heavens
towards the north ; but the next night it was
larger. It seemed to approach with fearful rapidity, from evening to evening, and, sweeping
in majesty across our western sky, disappeared
gradually in its progress towards the sun, around
which it whirled, and again appeared, more
faintly visible than before, just over our eastern
horizon, as if to give us one more glimpse of itself, a strange messenger of the Almighty, before

it passed off on its far-distant journey, not to return, until we, who are now young and free as air, are all laid quietly in the grave, or have become enfeebled and decrepid by the approach of age. Truly, great is God, who made the comet ; but to me, man also seems full of grandeur, when I find him capable of even *foretelling* the exact passage of such a body. Yet La Place enables any man to prophesy thus ; and in his "Mecanique Celeste" may you find all the elements necessary for this object. But he likewise tells us the forms of the planets ; he enables us to measure the ring which surrounds the planet Saturn, and even the form of the atmosphere surrounding the sun. In this same work he treats of those curious phenomena, which, as we see them daily, we think of little moment, the flow and ebb of the sea, or, in other words, high and low tides, and the causes of them. He treats of the motion of the earth about its centre, and the same motions in the moon and planets. These are the chief objects of the first and second volumes. The third volume, as we have already hinted, contains questions of great intricacy, and of immense importance ; namely, the exact motions of the planets around the sun, as affected

9

by all the attractions exerted upon them by the
various bodies of the universe; and the still
more important motions of our moon around
the earth; I say important, because the exact
knowledge of the course of this body is of the
greatest moment to every seaman who attempts
to go from one country to another, over the track-
less ocean. By means of observations upon this
planet, the sailor can sail over distant seas for
many months, and be able to return, when he
may wish, to his own home, in safety. Hence
the importance of the astronomer to the simple navigator of our planet. The history of
Dr. Bowditch is another proof of the truth of
this statement. By his accurate knowledge of
astronomy, by his ability to follow La Place, in
his investigations of all the motions of the solar
system, he was enabled to produce a work on
navigation which is sought for all over the world ;
as it combines the best methods of using the results of pure astronomy in the art of navigation.
The " Practical Navigator " would never have
maintained its hold upon the community as it
has done, if Dr. Bowditch had not been as skilful in mathematics and astronomy as in the details of navigation.

But to return to the "Mecanique Celeste."
The fourth volume contains similar investigations, namely, the motions of the satellites, or
moons, about the other planets. Of these, Jupiter's are the most interesting, after that of the
earth, or the moon. There are four of them.
These were the first that the invention of the
telescope, by Galileo, revealed to man ; and,
by their frequent revolutions around the planet,
they have in their turn shown to us many of the
laws, which govern the whole planetary system,
besides many curious and interesting facts in regard to their own forms and masses. From the
eclipses or disappearances of the first satellite,
when it passes on the side of the planet opposite
to that at which the observer from the earth is
looking, it has demonstrated the velocity of light.
Finally, the author treats of the seven moons,
or satellites, of Saturn, and likewise of the planet
Herschel, about which much less is known.

After attending to these subjects, La Place
investigates the powers which act upon comets,
which tend to turn from their courses those bodies, which, as I have before said, are flying in
very many directions throughout the universe,
and which are liable to be moved out of their

direction by the actions of some planets near which they may come. This was the case with a comet in 1770, whose course was wholly changed by the planet Jupiter drawing it towards its own body. To investigate the various laws of these disturbing forces is one object of this volume. Some other subjects are treated of; but of these I shall now not speak.

From this brief account of the " Mecanique Celeste," you may judge of the difficulties which the original writer had to overcome, in making it, and of the immense labor requisite. But La Place frequently supposes that a proposition is perfectly intelligible to his reader, because it is so to him. Having such a superior intellect, he is able to see that at a glance for which any one else would require a long demonstration, before he could become thoroughly master of the subject. The consequence of this is, an obscurity in the work, which has made it doubly difficult of comprehension. Several years ago, but a long time after Dr. Bowditch had read and made notes upon the whole work, an English writer said, that there were scarcely twelve men in Europe capable of comprehending it. Dr. Bowditch, feeling that it was the most impor-

tant work upon astronomy ever published, had
undertaken the translation of it, and had made
notes thereupon, for the purpose of " amusing
his leisure hours ; " and upon its being known
that he had finished the task, the American
Academy proposed to publish it at its own expense ; but Dr. Bowditch would not allow this,
and reserved the publication until he was able
to bring it forth with his own property.   But
let us see, now, what service Dr. B. intended
to perform by his translation and commentary.
His first object was to lay before America the
greatest work on the science of astronomy ever
published.   Secondly, his aim was to bring that
work down to the comprehension of young men
and students of mathematics, by filling up those
places left by La Place without demonstration.
Thirdly, he meant to give the history of the
science of astronomy for the last thirty years.
Fourthly, he wished to collect together all the
discoveries which he had made during the forty
years of his life that he had devoted to science.
His first aim was gained by the Translation.
His second was completely successful, for he was
assured by correspondents, both in America and
Europe, that he had enabled several to read the

immortal work of La Place, who never would
have done so, had not Dr. B. published his
Commentary. The Royal Astronomer at Pa-
lermo says, in a printed work, published after
the first two volumes of the Translation had
reached him, " Bowditch's Commentary should
be translated into Italian ; " and Lacroix, a celebrated French mathematician, advised a young
Swiss to read La Place in the American edition, rather than in the original. But what
pleased the commentator more than any thing
else, were the frequent letters from young men
residing in various parts of America, expressing
gratitude for the benefits they had received from
his work. When I think of these, I am reminded of the epithet bestowed upon Dr. Bowditch since his death, and by one well capable
of judging, namely, " Father of American Mathematics."   He has given a tone to the study of
science, which will be long felt.

In regard to the third object, all critics allow
that he was eminently successful in giving the
history of science up to the present time.

Upon the fourth point, we might refer, first,
to the immense increase of bulk of the work, as
a proof, but I prefer to mention a few details ;

and in order to this, let us examine the Commentary, and let it speak for itself. But it must be remembered, that, in making this examination, I must omit many circumstances, because you would not understand or feel interested in any greater detail.

In the first volume, he points out two errors of La Place, one of which relates to the motion of the earth ; and the other is of much importance. It relates to the permanency of our solar system, as it is commonly called. You all doubtless know, that the sun is situated in the centre, and the planets, with our earth, revolve around this luminary, which gives light and heat to all. Now, these bodies revolve in certain fixed " nearly circular " directions, and La Place thought that they would always continue to do so, and that Mercury, Venus, the Earth, Mars, Jupiter, Saturn, and Herschel, would for ever continue to wheel around in their accustomed orbits. Dr. Bowditch proves, however, that, though this may be true of the three larger planets, Jupiter, Saturn, and Herschel, it is not equally certain, *from the proofs given by La Place*, that our earth, or any of the other smaller planets, may not fly off into regions far remote from those in which they have been revolving for ages. This error had been made the subject of a paper to the American Academy at an earlier period of his life. But it must not be supposed that there is any proof that the solar system will not continue to exist for many long ages. On the contrary, there is no doubt that it will last millions of years. Dr. Bowditch merely wished to assert that La Place's argument and calculation did not prove as much as the French mathematician thought they did. In this volume Dr. Bowditch likewise alludes to a topic which he had made the subject of a communication, a long time previously, to the American Academy; I refer to a mistake in Newton's " Principia," which he discovered when quite young, and had sent an account of to the President of Harvard College. This gentleman transferred the question to the Professor of Mathematics, who believed the youth was mistaken. Doubtless, he thought it very strange that a simple youth should presume to correct any thing published by so eminent a man as Newton. The error of the Professor will become less singular, when you learn that the same mistake escaped the notice of all the commentators on the " Prin-

cipia," that is, for more than a century; and
that the cause of the original communication
being made to the Academy was the attempt of
Mr. Emerson, an Englishman, to prove the cor-
rectness of the English Philosopher. Every
one, I believe, now allows that Dr. Bowditch
was correct, and that a considerable error
would result, in calculating the orbit of a comet,
in using Newton's calculations.

CHAPTER XI.

Commentary continued : second volume. — Discussion between the English and French Mathematicians : Dr. B.'s
criticisms. — Errors in La Place, in regard to the earth,
&c. — Third volume : motions of the moon. — Fourth
volume : many errors discovered in it. — Halley's Comet. — Curious phenomena of capillary attraction.

In the second volume of the Commentary,
Dr. Bowditch makes very copious notes, in
which he shews a perfect knowledge of the works
of the chief mathematicians of Europe. He
stands as critic between two of the most powerful of the age ; Messrs. Ivory and Poisson ; the
former an Englishman, the latter a Frenchman,
and in reference, likewise, to a difficult subject
namely, the revolution or the turning of it upon
its own axis, as our earth does, of a fluid mass.
He not merely agrees with Mr. Poisson, but, by
a very simple illustration, proves the total inac-
curacy of Mr. Ivory's views. I well remember
the earnestness with which he studied this subject. Day after day, he returned to the task of
finding out some "simple case," with which to
prove to the satisfaction of others the truth of his
own view. At length, when he did discover it,

he jumped up in ecstacy, and, rubbing his hands and forehead with delight, exclaimed, " I have got it !"

Dr. Bowditch in this volume points out five errors or omissions made by La Place, some of which are very serious. One refers to the form of our earth, and had been previously communicated to the Academy. There is another, of some moment, relative to the time occupied in the revolution of one of Saturn's rings, La Place having made it longer than was true.

Finally, on the subject of the motion of the earth about its centre of gravity, he points out an error, in which La Place gives to two numbers only one third of their true value.

In the third volume, occupied as it is with the motions of the planets and of the moon, and with all the phenomena accompanying these, Dr. Bowditch shows much learning, and his power of bringing together all modern science. As in the previous volume, he labors without fear upon subjects treated of with much earnestness by La Place, Poisson, and Pontecoulant, in France, and Plana in Italy.

On the theory of the motions of the moon, a very difficult and interesting subject, Dr. B.

makes very copious notes, and the volume terminates with an appendix of more than two hundred and fifty pages, in which he gives the history of modern astronomy, in reference to the
calculations of the movements of planets and comets. In this, he speaks of Doctor Olbers and M.
Gauss. The former, from having discovered three
planets since eighteen hundred, is called " the
fortunate Columbus of the Heavens." The latter is one of the most remarkable men in the
world, for the rapidity with which he is able to
perform the most tedious and troublesome calculations.

We come now to the last volume, in printing
the thousandth page of which, he died. It was
the most difficult to him of the whole, and probably will raise him higher in the estimation of
the scientific world, than either of the others. In
the first place, I would remark, that, either from
the difficulty of the subject, or from the inatten-
tion of La Place, an unusual number of errors
was discovered. No less than twenty-four errors
or omissions are pointed out. Many of these seem
insignificant, but often, as may be supposed, they
materially affect the calculation. Most of them
refer to the derangements and the motions of Ju-

piter's satellites, a subject which occupies three
hundred and fourteen pages of the volume.   The
keenness of his criticism is again perceived upon
a subject in dispute between Plana and La Place,
and Dr. B. points out one mistake, and Poisson,
another, whereby Mr. Plana's views are proved
to coincide entirely with La Place's, instead of
being opposed to them.

I find a note upon Halley's comet, to which
I alluded, as presenting a grand spectacle in our
western sky, a few years since, and I cannot forbear mentioning the coincidence.   Dr. Bowditch, when making his notes upon the subject
of the motions and revolutions of comets, speaks
of Halley's comet, and mentions all that is known
about it, and its probable appearance.   This
note was prepared some time before it was printed.   It terminates thus : " Since writing the preceding part of this note, the comet has again appeared, and, *at the time of printing this page,
is visible in the heavens*, not far distant from the
place corresponding to the elements of Mr. Pontecoulant."

The work, so far as Dr. B. is concerned, fin-
ishes with the most curious and difficult subject
of capillary attraction, or that power whereby a

liquid arises in narrow tubes beyond the level of the fluid outside, as we see familiarly in sponges, and cloths, and hollow pieces of glass. You may think this subject of little moment ; yet La Place thought it more curious than almost any other, and he calls the attention of mathematicians to it, with much earnestness. You would scarcely suppose that the dewdrop, that glitters on the grass in the morning, would suggest ideas to the philosopher about the formation of a planet : yet so it is. The same laws, which govern the gathering together of the bright drops of water, have bound together the particles of our earth. Of course, such a subject would call forth the best minds. After La Place, came Gauss, whose results were similar to those of La Place. But, in 1831, Mr. Poisson, the first mathematician now living,* of whom we have already spoken frequently, put forth a work, wherein he pretends to have produced many new views on the subject, by taking into consideration certain particulars which La Place did not. Dr. Bowditch received this work while engaged in printing this volume. He ceased printing, and devoted six months or more to a thorough perusal of the new

* Since this was written Poisson has died.

French work ; and the result has been, that he has proved that, without an exception, unless where an evident error was made by La Place, the principles of this mathematician, when fairly carried out, would produce all the results which Mons. Poisson has given as new in his work ; thereby, in fact, putting aside entirely the new theory of capillary attraction, brought forward by the living philosopher. This is decidedly the most important part of the work, so far as Dr. Bowditch is concerned. It places him much higher than before in the scale of mathematical rank.

I would willingly give a further analysis, but I forbear, because it would not be interesting to you. It was in correcting this, his noblest task, in the plenitude of his strength of intellect, that he was destined to die.

CHAPTER XII.

Sketch of the life of La Grange, the equal of La Place :
love Dr. B. had for this person's character : comparison
between him and La Place : also between him and Dr.
Bowditch. — Conclusion of the Memoir.

DURING this history, I frequently have
spoken of different individuals; but there is
one, about whom little mention has been
made, but of whose life I wish to give you a
short history, as his character resembles very
much that of Dr. Bowditch. His mind and
heart were always regarded by the American
mathematician with feelings of respect and love,
such as he felt towards no other philosopher.
An equal, too, of La Place, it seems not im-
proper to mention him, and I know you will
excuse the slight interruption in my story, when
you perceive how this lofty nature of La Grange
seems to harmonize with and to illustrate as it
were the life of Dr. Bowditch.

Joseph Louis La Grange, one of the most
famous geometricians of modern times, was born
at Turin, January 25, 1736.   He was one of
eleven children of parents who became very

poor, so that Joseph had in early life to gain his own subsistence. When young, he devoted himself to the classics, and read Latin constantly. At seventeen his taste for abstruse mathematics first showed itself, and from this period he continued studying by himself, without aid, and in two years he had acquired a knowledge of all that was known upon the science, and began to correspond with the geometricians of other lands. In 1755, he sent to Euler, then the greatest in the world, and residing in Berlin, an answer to a problem proposed by Euler, ten years before, to the learned men of Europe, and which they had been unable to solve. Meanwhile, he was appointed Professor of Mathematics at Turin, at the age of nineteen years, and soon afterwards originated the academy of sciences at that place; and in their Memoirs he published papers, in which he not merely criticised Euler and D'Alembert, and others but brought forward some very curious new views of science, discovered by himself. Europe soon resounded with his praises, and he was chosen member of all the learned societies. In 1766, he was called to the Court of Frederick the Great, of Prussia, to take the place of Euler, who was summoned

10

by the Emperor of Russia to St. Petersburg.
Frederick wrote to him thus : " Come to my
Court, for it is right that the greatest mathematician in Europe should be near the greatest king."
He remained there until Frederick died, and soon
after that he was invited by the French government to come to Paris.   From this time, with
slight interruptions, his fame continued to increase, and every one delighted to honor him ;
for his labors did honor to his adopted country.
One of the most beautiful compliments, perhaps,
ever paid to man, was the message sent by the
French government to the venerable father of
La Grange, at Piedmont, when that country
fell by a revolution, under French influence.
" Go," said the Minister of Foreign Affairs, to
his ambassador, " go to the venerable father of
the illustrious La Grange, and say to him, that,
after the events that have just taken place, the
French Government look to him as the first object of their interest."   The answer of the old
man was touching : " This day is the happiest
of my life, and my son is the cause of it ! "   And
thrice blessed must be such a son ! for he fills
the last hours of his father's life with peace.
When Bonaparte came into power, new honors

were showered upon him. But what was it that charmed Dr. Bowditch, in the character of La Grange? It was the combination of a giant intellect with extreme modesty and simplicity, a sincere love of truth, and almost feminine affections. He was a pure being, whose intellect equalled La Place's, but who at the same time was full of the utmost gentleness and strict justice. He was at Berlin during the earlier part of La Place's career in Paris. In after-life, the two were friends. Both were great geniuses; both were capable of the highest flights of thought, and of bringing down to the comprehension of mankind the vast and wise laws impressed by God on the system of the universe. But La Place soiled his reputation by trifling political ambition. La Grange stood aside, quiet and pleased with his own high thoughts; yet, if his fellows wished him to take upon himself any public duties, he took them cheerfully, and as cheerfully resigned them. La Place courted honors; La Grange meekly received them. La Place had few to love him, for he stripped others of the fruits of their labors, to cover himself with their glory; but in the heart of La Grange sat humility, justice, and philan-

thropic love. In fact, La Grange was full of
the loftiest virtue and genius, while La Place
had the latter, merely. Such were two men
whose works Dr. Bowditch read with the greatest pleasure. But he often spoke with great
feeling of the noble traits in the character of La
Grange. The features and form of the head of
Dr. Bowditch resembled those of the French
astronomer; and I have often thought, that, as
they were like each other in countenance, so
their dispositions and fortunes in life were more
nearly similar than is usual in this world. Both
were born poor, and early had to seek subsistence for themselves. Each devoted himself
early to the science of mathematics; and both
became eminent in it. Love of truth, and a
longing for it, every where, were strong traits in
both; order and regularity of life, and simplicity of food and regimen, belonged to them
equally. Above all, a sincere reverence for
goodness, for true modesty and delicate refine-
ment, and a deep respect for the female sex,
were strikingly manifest in both. They were
moderate in their desires. They had the highest good of humanity at heart. Both sought
for quiet and retirement from the turmoil of life,

in their " peaceful mathematics." As the lives
of both were beautiful, so was the serenity of
their death scenes. I shall terminate this short
story of La Grange, by a few details of his
death. He was attacked near the end of March
1813 by a severe fever, and the symptoms soon
became alarming. He saw the danger he was
in, but preserved still his serenity of soul. " I
am studying," says he, " what is passing within
me, as if I were now engaged in some great and
rare experiment." On the eighth of April, his
friends, Messrs. Lacepede, Monge, and Chap-
tal, visited him, and, in a long conversation
which he entered into with them, he showed
that his memory was still unclouded, and his intellect as bright as ever. He spoke to them of
his actual condition, of his labors, of his success, of the tenor of his life ; and expressed no
regret at dying, except at the idea of being separated from his wife, whose kind attentions had
been unremittingly bestowed upon him. He
soon sunk, and died. Three days afterwards,
his body was deposited in the Pantheon, as it is
called, the great burial place for the renowned
men of France ; and La Place, and his friend
Lacepede, delivered their tributes of praise and

admiration over his grave. So peaceful and
calm was the death of him whose life 1 have
been trying to place before you.

Dr. Bowditch's health had been generally
good, though he never was robust. In 1808,
he was dangerously ill, with a cough, and, by
the advice of a physician, he took a journey.
He first went towards Pawtucket and Provi-
dence; thence, westerly, through Hartford and
New Haven, as far as Albany, and back again,
across the interior of Massachusetts, as far as
the fertile valley of the Connecticut river.
Thence, passing upwards, he crossed on the
southern borders of Vermont and New Hampshire, to Newburyport, and back to Salem.
This journey quite restored him, and he never
afterwards suffered much from cough ; and very
generally enjoyed good health, until his last illness.   He sometimes continued, however, for a
long while, without any complaint of suffering ;
for he was unwilling to trouble his friends with
any detail of his illness.

In 1834, his wife died. His heart was borne
down by the loss. She had been to him always a
loving and a tender companion ; faithful and true,
even to the minutest points. She had watched

all his labors. She had urged him onward in the pursuit of science, by telling him that she would find the means of meeting any expense, by her own economy, in her care of the family. She had watched the progress of his greatest work which, with his dying hands, he afterwards dedicated to her memory. She had listened with delight to all the praises that had come to him, from his own countrymen and foreign lands; and now, when he was full of honor and yet active in business, she was called to leave him. With her, the real charm of life departed, and many sad hours would have been the consequence, if his sense of duty, and devotion to study, had not prevented them. He devoted himself now more closely to active engagements. He always spoke of his wife with extreme fondness, and sometimes his tears flowed afresh. There was a degree of sadness, which was perceptible only to his family, however, that settled upon Dr. Bowditch during the last four years of life, in consequence of this deprivation.

In the latter part of the summer and early days of autumn of 1837, he began to feel that he was losing strength, and had occasionally pains of great severity. He continued his employments, however, without yielding to suffering. In January, 1838, he submitted to medical advice ; but it was of no avail. He sunk rapidly, under a severe and torturing disease, which, for the last fortnight of life, deprived him of the power of eating, or even of drinking any thing, except a small quantity of wine and water. Until the last moment of his life, he was engaged in attending to the duties of the Life Office, and to the publication of his Commentary on the " Mecanique Celeste." During this time, after he lost the power of visiting State Street, he used to walk into his library, and there sit down among his beloved books, and pass the hours in gentle conversation with his friends, of each one of whom he seemed very anxious to take a last farewell. He received them in succession, during the forenoon ; and towards those whom he loved particularly, he showed his tenderness by kissing them when they met and when they parted. His conversation with them was of the most elevated kind. He told them of his prospects of death, of his past life, and of his perfect calmness, and reliance on God. He spoke to them of his love of moral worth. " Talents without goodness I care little for," said he to one of them. With his children he was always inexpressibly affectionate. "Come, my dears," said he, "I fear you will think me very foolish, but I cannot help telling you all how much I love you ; for whenever any of you approach me, I feel as if I had a fountain of love which gushes out upon you." He spoke to them, at the dead of the night, when he awoke, pleasant as a little child, yet with the bright, clear mind of a philosopher. He told them of his life, of his desire always to be innocent, to be active in every duty, and in the acquirement of knowledge ; and then alluded to a motto that he had impressed upon his mind in early life, that a good man must have a happy death. On one of these occasions he said, "I feel now quiet and happy, for I think my life has been somewhat blameless."

It was noon, and all was quiet in his library. A bright ray of light streamed through the half closed shutter ; he was calm and free from pain. One of his children bade him good-bye for a time. Stretching out his hand and pointing to the sunlight, he said, "Good-bye, my son, the work is done ; and if I knew I were to be gone when the sun sleeps in the west, I would say, 'thy will, oh God, be done.'" Observing some around him weeping, while he was quiet, he quoted his favorite passage from Hafez, one of the sweetest of the poets of Persia :

> " So live that, sinking in thy last long sleep,
>   Calm thou may'st smile while all around thee weep."

On another similar occasion, when one who was near him had a sad countenance, he told her to be cheerful, and then taking Bryant's Poems he read the four last verses of that exquisite little poem called the " Old Man's Funeral." It is so beautiful in itself, that I want you to read it, and perhaps you may like to see how he thought it applied to his own condition. I have placed in parentheses his remarks.

THE OLD MAN'S FUNERAL.

I saw an aged man upon his bier,
   His hair was thin and white, and on his brow
A record of the cares of many a year ;
   Cares that were ended and forgotten now.
And there was sadness round, and faces bowed,
And women's tears fell fast, and children wailed aloud.

Then rose another hoary man and said,
   In faltering accents to that weeping train,
Why mourn ye that our aged friend is dead ?
   Ye are not sad to see the gathered grain,
Nor when their mellow fruit the orchards cast,
Nor when the yellow woods shake down the ripened mast.

Ye sigh not when the sun, his course fulfilled,
  His glorious course, rejoicing earth and sky,
In the soft evening, when the winds are stilled,
  Sinks where his islands of refreshment lie,
And leaves the smile of his departure spread
O'er the warm-colored heaven, and ruddy mountain head.

Why weep ye then for him, who, having won
  The bound of man's appointed years, at last,
Life's blessings all enjoyed, life's labors done,
  Serenely to his final rest has past;
          [I cannot agree to the next two lines.]
While the soft memory of his virtues, yet
Lingers like twilight hues, when the bright sun is set."

His youth was innocent; [yes, I believe mine was inno-
          cent; not guilty, certainly.] his riper age,
  Marked with some act of goodness every day, [no, not
          every day — sometimes.]
And watched by eyes that loved him, calm and sage, [oh,
          yes, watched by eyes that loved him, and oh! how
          calm, but I cannot add, sage.]
  Faded his late declining years away.
Cheerful he gave his being up, and went
To share [he hopes] the holy rest that waits a life [he hopes]
          well spent.

That life was happy; every day he gave
  Thanks for the fair existence that was his; [yes, every
          morning when I awoke, and saw the beautiful sun
          rise, I thanked God that he had placed me in this
          beautiful world.]
For a sick fancy made him not her slave,
  To mock him with her phantom miseries.

No chronic tortures racked his aged limb,
For luxury and sloth had nourished none for him. [yes,
            that is all true.]

And I am glad that he has lived thus long,
    And glad that he has gone to his reward;
Nor deem that kindly nature did him wrong,
    Softly to disengage the vital cord. [Oh, how softly, how
            sweetly is the cord disengaging!]
When his weak hand grew palsied, and his eye
Dark with the mists of age, it was his time to die. [Yes,
            it was his time to die; remember this; do not
            look sad or mournful, it is his time to die.]

One of the curious effects of his illness was his
new love for flowers.   He had never shown any
great pleasure in them during life, although the
rose, or lilly of the valley were frequently in his
vest during the summer.   One day during his
illness, Miss —— sent him a nosegay, in the
centre of which was a white camelia japonica.
" Ah! how beautiful!" he exclaimed, " tell her
how much I am pleased; place them where I
can see them.   Tell her that the japonica is to
me the emblem of her spotless heart."   Music
too, as it had been his delight in early life, now
served to soothe his last hours.   One evening,
when surrounded by his family, and he was free
from all pain, the door of the library was suddenly
opened, and his favorite tune of Robin Adair was

heard richly swelling from some musical glasses in the entry.   Its plaintiveness was always delightful to him ; and after listening to it till it died away, he exclaimed, " O, how beautiful ! I feel as if I should like to have the tune that I have loved in life prove my funeral dirge."

It was on the fifteenth of March, 1838, that being too feeble to walk, he was drawn for the last time into the library.   On the next day he was confined to the bed.   On that day a beautiful incident took place, which I cannot forbear to mention.   He had called his daughter his Jessamine, and about twenty-four hours before his death, she obtained for him that delicate white flower.   He took it, and kissed it many times. He then returned it with these words : " Take it, my love ; it is beautiful ; it is the queen of flowers.   Let it be for you, forever, the emblem of truth and of purity.   Let it be the Bowditch arms.   Place it in your mother's Bible, and by the side of La Place's bust ; and to-morrow, if I am alive, I will see it."

In the evening he drew a little water into his parched mouth.   " How delicious," he murmured.   " I have swallowed a drop from

> ' Siloa's brook that flow'd
> Fast by the oracle of God.' "

On the morrow he died.   Had he lived nine
days more, he would have exactly completed
his sixty-fifth year.   On the next Sabbath he
was laid quietly by the side of his wife, Mary.
As his body was carried towards the spot, gentle snow-flakes fell upon it, fit emblems, they
seemed to be, of his purity.

CPSIA information can be obtained
at www.ICGtesting.com
Printed in the USA
BVOW08s1957300317
479900BV00001B/36/P